P. C. Croll

Ancient and historic landmarks in the Lebanon Valley

P. C. Croll

Ancient and historic landmarks in the Lebanon Valley

ISBN/EAN: 9783742827142

Manufactured in Europe, USA, Canada, Australia, Japa

Cover: Foto ©ninafisch / pixelio.de

Manufactured and distributed by brebook publishing software
(www.brebook.com)

P. C. Croll

Ancient and historic landmarks in the Lebanon Valley

Truly Yours,
P. C. Croll.

CONTENTS.

(iii)

PREFACE.

THE author desires to say to his gentle reader that when he began to pen the contents of this volume he had no desire to write a book. Seeing a volume of interesting local history lie at his feet, he began to open it and read. Then he became inclined to impart the information gained unto others, and hence chose as his vehicle one of the daily papers of his own city. In *The Daily Report* appeared, for seven months, from January to August, 1894, in consecutive order, under the *nom de plume* of "Kristofer Kolumbo," these weekly contributions. They soon attracted attention, and wherever among readers the author's name became known, he was besought to gather the material into permanent and convenient form. He has therefore no apology to make for its appearance in this way. He has but yielded to a general local demand to preserve what historic matter these fugitive sketches may contain.

To aid the general reader now undertaking this imaginary historical pilgrimage, a number of illustrations have been secured for these pages. The letters the author prefers to stand substantially as they were first written, asking simply that the reader bear in mind that they are

(vii)

"Letters." If they should induce any one to make an actual pilgrimage to this ancient settlement, to see for himself these landmarks and study them "face to face," the writer entertains no fear of ever hearing any regrets from such an one for the undertaking.

The article on Womelsdorf is here inserted in its proper place, though it was last written, and this accounts for its midsummer flavor, the season when these contributions were brought to their termination.

We hope new readers may find something to please and instruct.

P. C. C.

LEBANON, PA., *March, 1895.*

INTRODUCTION.

THIS book commends itself. Its publication is in response to a demand. Its contents were first published in a series of articles in a Lebanon daily paper. The reading of these articles created much interest, and resulted in a general desire to have the material in more permanent form. It was the expression of this desire, mainly, that led the modest author to the idea of the book.

The book will be read with more than ordinary interest. It is the story of the early settlement of central Pennsylvania. The story is told in a sprightly way that makes it attractive. The material was gathered with much labor, and substantiated by personal investigation. It contains many incidents in the early history of this section, both in its secular affairs and in its church work, not elsewhere to be found.

The book will be valuable as a reference. The section of territory which it covers was the scene of some of the most important events in the early settlement of the State. Associated with them is the name of Conrad Weiser. If the life and deeds of this man were properly known, his name would scarcely stand second to any in

2   (ix)

the roll of worthies of the Commonwealth. He was the
valued associate and adviser of men high in authority
in affairs civil and ecclesiastical. Many of these events
have no record. They exist simply in traditions handed
down from generation to generation. With the lapse
of time these are becoming dim and indistinct. It is
important that they should have a record in permanent
form.

The book can not fail to be of interest, not only to
those now living in this section, but also to those who
have gone forth from it to settle other sections. The
descendants of the people who took part in these scenes
are to be found in every part of the country. They fill
all ranks of life. Many of them have inherited and
carried with them the spirit of their earnest and daring
ancestors, and have become leaders in thought and life
and enterprise in their chosen communities. This
book ought to be in the hands of every man and woman
who traces back ancestry to the early settlers of central
Pennsylvania.

The book opens a field that is rich in material and
that ought to be developed. Its publication is timely.
The Lutheran Publication Society is to be commended
for giving it to the general public. The Pennsylvania
German has been altogether too modest. Conservative
almost to a fault, he has not cared to herald his deeds
to fame. By reason of this same conservatism, he has
furnished to our social, civil and ecclesiastical life, an
element of stability and strength. We have the record

in detail of the history of the New England settlements. We rejoice in it as a common heritage of glory. The New Englander is properly proud of his Puritan ancestry. When once the record of our Pennsylvania settlements shall be given in detail, we will have reason to be equally proud of our German ancestry.

We rejoice in the organization of the "Pennsylvania German Society." It has a history back of it which ought to inspire the most devout enthusiasm. It has a high and holy duty to perform in creating new interest in that history. We commend this book to the members of this society. Its contents will be an impetus to more extended research. Its reading ought to lead some gifted historian to take up and follow the lines here laid down, and to put in permanent and systematic form the records of the deeds of these brave and devoted people to whom we owe so much.

To those interested in the history of the Lutheran Church in this country these sketches will be of special value. Directly or indirectly, the events are very closely identified or connected with the church-life of the time. It is interesting to note how one of the first acts of the German settlers was to establish a church. It is significant to note how that church became the center of the life of the settlement. There are many facts here recorded of very great interest in the annals of our early church history.

The peculiar value of the book consists in the fact

that it gives us glimpses of the inner home-life and church-life of the time. We see the godly pastor making his way among the scattered settlements, visiting the widely separated homes, sitting with the family gathered around the unpretentious board. We see the congregation gathering from their distant homes, assembling in the plain and comfortless, yet to them none the less sacred structures, to worship God and to listen in reverent attention to the preached truth. Now and then there comes a revelation of the devout spirit and the sturdy piety and the rugged faith of these people. It will do us good to recall and study these times, to catch some of the spirit of earnestness and simplicity in life and devotion.

W. H. DUNBAR.

BALTIMORE, *March, 1855.*

ANCIENT AND HISTORICAL

LANDMARKS IN THE LEBANON VALLEY.

CHAPTER I.

A BIRD'S-EYE VIEW OF THE VALLEY.

I PROPOSE to lead my readers in a leisurely conducted excursion through the rich and well-cultivated valley, which furnishes a general and, we trust, a happy home to most of them. The object of these rambles shall be to lead to the historic and the antique, in which this locality abounds, if indeed anything may be called ancient in this our western country, save its rocks and hills, its forests and its water-ways.

Although it is less than two centuries since our present blooming valley was still the exclusive dominion of the Indians and their sometimes less savage neighbors, the wild beasts, and only since that time that the foot of the white settler first stepped upon its soil, yet we are wont to speak of the rude relics left us by these first settlers—our ancestors—as ancient. Their primitive structures—whether they be houses or barns, churches or forts, mills or furnaces—over which a hun-

dred and fifty years or more of varied weather has beaten
down, many of which have clustering about them interesting and important facts of history, while some
bid fair to defy the gnawing tooth of time for another
equally lengthy period—these ancient relics hold for us
an enticing charm, and it is in quest of them that we
shall undertake our pilgrimage.

We shall take our weekly strolls on successive Satur-
days, partly because it furnishes a half-holiday to many
toilers, whom we would fain have accompany us, and
because it enables the rising generation, our school
children, for whose especial benefit these excursions
are taken, to join the party. For we shall take these
rambles now, while the schools are in session, in the
hope that when vacation comes it may lead some
bands of bright historians or juvenile "Old Mortalitys"
to visit these spots in reality, and retrace anew the fading epitaphs upon the moss-covered sandstones that
mark the resting places of our earliest local pioneers.
Therefore, as our present trip is taken in imagination's
chariot, we shall allow no interruptions to interfere with
this weekly trip, though "Old Prob." should decree to
take vengeance upon us and impede our way with snow-
banks or howling blizzards before the wintry season be
o'er. Our flying Pegasus must carry us over all these.
Only the touch of Providence upon the hand of the guide
can stay his pencil, which shall serve as our wand.

Before we undertake the journey, however, we will
take a bird's-eye glimpse of the territory we are about to

traverse. It is possible that most of our readers have before gone up and down our Lebanon Valley from Reading to Harrisburg. Perhaps they took their trip in private conveyance, or stage-coach, or old-fashioned "tally-ho," over the well-kept turnpike, that has for 78 years conducted visitors in rumbling coaches through the very heart of this district. Perhaps they have taken a trip on some canal-boat that formerly plied its way along the circuitous route of the Union canal, the first to be operated in America, and abandoned only in 1884. Many, I know, have employed that more modern and speedy and comfortable mode of locomotion, the Philadelphia and Reading express train, and have been whirled through this garden land of our State. It is possible that some have taken this trip afoot, and others still have wheeled through it on a Victor or a Columbia. Future travelers will doubtless make the journey by electricity, perhaps at no distant day on wheels, when the Lebanon and Annville street railway shall extend its lines to either terminus, or on wings, when Mr. Edison shall have completed his electrical flying-machine.

But to-day we shall soar upwards with the eagle. Having no balloon at hand large enough to accommodate my many passengers, I shall ask each one gracefully to spread the pinions of his fancy while we soar away to the height of a few hundred yards, and look down upon our bustling valley as the swallows and the eagles do in summer. And we shall imagine it to be summer, to see the country clothed in its harvest riches and glory, as the writer saw it some years since, from one of the highest peaks that hem it in on the south.

And now look to the east and west, to the north and south! What a magnificent country lies beneath you! Above the din of its noises let the valley's enrapturing beauty and boundless magnificence transport your soul! Let the extensive picture daguerreotype itself upon your mind and heart! What an empire of fertile farms! On and on the billowy fields are rolling, clad in the wealth of emerald beauty! On and on the terrestrial billows of this sea are flowing, one farm lashing against another, until ten miles to the north it strikes against its Blue Mountain promontory, while to the south this agricultural sea breaks itself up in green undulations of woodland against the spurs of our South Mountain range. Between the Schuylkill on the east and the Susquehanna on the west there is no break or limit to our vision. Beyond these borders, even, the eye can discern mountain ranges in the hazy distance.

But what do we see in this broad expanse beneath our feet? Immediately beneath us lies the queen of the valley, the proud young city of Lebanon itself, with a girdle of industries around her waist, alas! now in part idle, and a crown of copper and iron upon her Cornwallian brow, alas! now so poorly burnished! Around this enthroned queen, on every hand, extending far as the eye can see, lie the rich and improved acres of our people, the best legacy which our German sires have left their sons and descendant heirs. The log cabins of the first

settlers have in most instances been displaced by commodious farm-houses, many of them palatial structures
of stone or brick, whose domestic comfort and attraction
lure the most fastidious. And what barns! No community on earth can boast of finer and larger barns than
these "Switzers" of our Lebanon valley Pennsylvania-
German georgic princes. Yet such is the skill of this
king of farmers, the Pennsylvania-German, that even
these gigantic storehouses are often known to overflow
with farm products, and rows of hive-shaped stacks of
hay and grain have to be set near by, as so many sentinels to guard the rich farm treasures.

Studding this valley, from the east to the west, are
still preserved a sufficient number of significant landmarks to make our pilgrimage interesting. These are
in the form of old churches and cemeteries, Indian forts
and ancient dwellings, battlefields and illustrious graves,
which we shall visit with sacred veneration, and by the
aid of our magic wand call up the dead from their graves,
re-people the old dwellings, and, in short, rehabilitate
the old scenes with actors and environments of a generation that has passed away long ago. We shall cover especially that district now included in the limits of ·
Lebanon county or bordering close thereto. So, if you
will join the party, gentle reader, be ready for our first
tramp just a week from now. Until then, and in the
hope of your landing upon *terra firma* from your aerial
flight, more safely than did the famous Darius Green with
his flying machine, we will separate for a brief season.

CHAPTER II.

CONRAD WEISER'S HOMESTEAD AND GRAVE.

WELL, here we meet again! Our flying steed has been restlessly pawing up the air for a week, eager to make the first trip of exploration promised in my former communication. So, if all my passengers are ready, I shall give the word to start. Therefore, *all aboard*, and we'll be off.

Inasmuch as we shall confine our excursions, for the present at least, as nearly as is practicable, to the territory covered by our present county limits, we will take our first trip eastward, and begin our research just beyond the county-line, and from thence work upward and westward toward home. I shall, therefore, to-day lead my readers to the almost sacred shrine of the present resting-place and former home of that famous, heroic, and many-sided and gifted pioneer of this valley, whose name deserves easily to stand first among the illustrious ancestors of this later generation, Conrad Weiser. Were due justice given this German hero and patriot, his name would doubtless stand among the first which our State has chosen to blazon upon her scroll of honor.

Our best way to reach this historic spot is by taking

the well-kept pike and keeping on, until 14 miles to the
East, we come to Womelsdorf, one of the first built
towns of this valley, and about fifty years ago a most
prosperous place of business, its stores then rivaling
those of Reading. Passing through this borough and a
quarter of a mile beyond, we come to a lane leading to
the right, where, just across a meadow-field, cluster the
capacious farm dwellings of the Weiser Homestead, now

CONRAD WEISER'S HOMESTEAD.

in the possession and occupancy of Mr. John Marshall.
This courteous gentleman will be glad to show us what
is of such intense interest here. First he will show us
the old stone dwelling, which Weiser built early in the

last century, but still kept intact. Although it is kept
as a wash and slaughter-house, and for general storage
purposes, yet we wander through it with bated breath.
Curiosity holds sway over us as we travel from garret to
basement, whither these early Tulpehocken settlers fled

ANOTHER VIEW OF THE CONRAD WEISER HOMESTEAD.

for refuge, and where we find a huge Queen Anne
mantel-piece of solid oak, still as in the days when Maria
Weiser (Conrad's eldest daughter, who later became the
wife of that patriarch of the American Lutheran Church,
Heinrich Melchoir Muhlenberg), there kindled the fires.
We look at the quaint old structure with its low door,

and almost imagine this illustrious pair coming forth as bride and groom on that day in 1745, when they went to the Tulpehocken Lutheran parsonage, to be united in the sacred bonds of matrimony, by the pastor, Rev. Tobias Wagner.

We repair to the present farm house, and are glad, among other relics, to look at a parchment deed or patent of land given the original settler by the Penn heirs, John, Richard and Thomas Penn. Then we walk to the sacred spot that holds the dust of the illustrious and pious German pioneer of this valley. A plain sandstone is the only marker this grave has, though we are glad to say that an effort is now on foot by the public schools of Berks county, headed by its energetic Superintendent, Prof. W. M. Zechman, to put up at an early day a suitable monument to Weiser's honor in the city of Reading. This movement has been seconded by the Board of Trade of Reading, and by the Pennsylvania-German Society at its last annual meeting. It thus bids fair soon to be realized.

The Weiser burial plot is a patch of ground about forty feet square, not more than fifty yards removed from the old house, on a slight elevation of ground in the midst of a thriving orchard of apple trees. Here lie buried possibly a dozen different members of the Weiser family, together with a few Indians. Only the tombstone of Conrad and his wife (rather that of the wife of a son by the same name, as dates do not correspond with the marriage of the elder Conrad with his Anna Eva, whom tradition will make out to have been a squaw) are found remaining. Other graves are marked by broken or well-nigh buried lime-stone slabs. The epi-

CONRAD WEISER'S GRAVE.

taph on Mr. Weiser's tombstone, recently retraced from its fading indistinctness under the ravages of Father Time's influences for nearly a century and a half, reads follows:

Diesea ist
die Ruhe Staetle
des weyl Ehren
Geachteu M. CON-
RADI WEISERS.   Der-
aelbige GebohreN
1696 D. 2 November
in ASTAET im Amt
HerreNBerg, in Wit-
tenberger LANDE.
Und Gestorben
1760 D. 13 Julius.
Ist Alt Worden
64 Jahr 3 M. 3 W. 6 T.

This grave has been visited by many men and women since that eminent man was buried here, 134 years ago. Hither the illustrious families of Weiser and Muhlenberg and Shulze (including the once Governor of Pennsylvania) and other descendants of fame have made their pilgrimages in respect to a worthy sire. But perhaps the most illustrious personage that ever visited the spot was President George Washington, who, during his second term of office, visited Womelsdorf and this grave, coming from Philadelphia. It was on November 13 and 14, 1793, spending the intervening night in Womelsdorf, where he was serenaded by the citizens on the evening of the 13th. The reply to this greeting of the citizens is still preserved, and can be found in Rupp's history. The visit to Conrad Weiser's grave was made on the morning of the 14th, we think, and doubtless with due thought of, perhaps in company with the illustrious grandson of Weiser, General Peter Muhlenberg, who, in various battles of the Revolution gave such gallant and signal service to the great leader of the colonial forces.

It would be interesting to lead the reader into the very interesting sketch of this Pennsylvania German leader in church and civil affairs, but we are rather interested now in historic landmarks than in biography. Besides, the general reader knows the honored *role* this man played. Let it suffice to say that our State furnished no character, not even the illustrious Franklin excepted, with whom he was frequently associated in public service, who, in that colonial period of our history, did so much for the amicable settlement of land disputes with the aboriginal Indians as Weiser did. Where Penn made one famous treaty, this man made scores, only alas! for the poor German's future reputation, they were never blazoned so conspicuously on the pages of our histories. In every significant dispute or settlement of lands with the Indians from Albany, N. Y., to Richmond, Va., between 1732 and 1760, it is safe in assuming that Conrad Weiser played a prominent part. Now we find him with Benjamin Franklin, at Albany, N. Y., attending the first conference for Colonial Federation; now with Governor Dinwiddie, of Virginia, settling a dispute and acting as Indian interpreter. Again we see him settling church disputes and healing factions in his own Tulpehocken Lutheran field; and then he travels with Count Zinzendorf to Shamokin (now Sunbury) and aids in the establishment of a Christian mission there among the Indians. At one time he is at the head of a regiment of German farmers, armed with flint-locks, pitch-forks, etc., marching against the invading French and Indian foes, and leading them all through the length of our valley from Reading to the Susquehanna. At another time he is in correspondence with Governor Morris for state aid and protection. Now he is a plain farmer in his Heidelberg homestead, which was a landmark already in 1740, and known on old maps simply as "Weisers;" then we find him as merchant or jurist in the city of Reading, or else assisting in laying out its streets.

So, while we turn away from this grave, we know we have stood above the dust of a truly great man, for whose life our German people especially, and all the State as well, should ever feel a profound respect and grateful indebtedness.

In the next chapter we shall pay a visit to the ancient town of Womelsdorf, founded by a relative of Weiser, and located on the edge of Weiser's original farm.

3

CHAPTER III.

MIDDLETOWN ALIAS WOMELSDORF.

LESS than half a mile to the west of Conrad Weiser's homestead and grave, situated on part of this pioneer's original farm of one thousand acres, and on the Berks and Dauphin turnpike, well shaded by an abundance of lindens and other copiously foliaged trees, nestles the healthy and handsome little town of Womelsdorf, formerly known as Middletown, because situated midway between the early advancing and out-striding towns of Reading and Lebanon. It is laid out on rolling ground, thus enabling the slightest rain to carry off every vestige of filth and decay from its streets into a streamlet of purest spring-water that flows by its base, and because of which superior surface drainage, it enjoys the reputation of being one of the healthiest towns in Eastern Pennsylvania. Its streets are regularly laid out, and. the chief of them are lined with comfortable, and in a few instances, with elegant and palatial residences. These qualities, together with its quiet and its beautiful rural scenery and its close proximity to the mountains, (a spur of the South Mountain Ridge), and its many springs of excellent water, have made it a rendezvous in summer months for a considerable number of former

(26)

residents and their friends, who, when the dog-days drive them from their sweltering city homes, hie away to its cool abodes and shady streets. Thus it comes that modern Womelsdorf is quite a summer resort, and that every year a certain increasing number of pilgrims (the scions of old residents here), wend their pilgrimage towards this Mecca, and enroll themselves among its midsummer guests. Nor have these any cause to regret their choice, based upon any inferiority in the social or intellectual qualities of its present citizens.

So much for modern Womelsdorf. But we seek to explore the olden village of Middletown, and must, therefore, enter its ancient highway and walk along its original thoroughfares. An old map shows that one of the first roads of this portion of the county led from the Schuylkill Ford (where Reading now is located) to Weiser's, and past his residence on beyond the Blue Mountains, by way of Rehrersburg on to Sunbury. This road led past the Conrad Weiser home, just one field's breadth south of the present pike, and entered the town, as now built, through the corner lot of Mrs. Rev. Chas. Leinbach, obliquely across the pike where Mr. Fogelman's residence is now located, past an old hostelry that used to stand on the fine lot of Mr. Harry Fidler, on across present building lots to where the present Rehrersburg road branches off from Franklin or "Blue" street. From this main thoroughfare two streets ran north and south, known by the suggestive names of "Schmalz-gass" and "Gnocken-strose." Along these old streets are found to-day the oldest architectural landmarks in the shape of low, one-roomed, one-storied log cabins. Some of them have been repaired and remodelled into convenient and more modern looking homes, while a few have been left undisturbed under the ravaging influence of time and weather since their

SCHMALZ-GASS, WOMELSDORP.

first erection, more than a century and a quarter ago. One of the best specimens of this latter class is the dilapidated log-hut at the corner of Franklin street and Rehrersburg road, at present owned and occupied by Mrs. Williams, a soldier's widow, and another widow

woman by the name of McDonough. The most interesting historic association attached to this old building
is the fact that the same is pointed out as the place
where the celebrated Baron Henry W. Stiegel, of Manheim fame, when reduced in his worldly circumstances,
ended his days in poverty, teaching an old-time school.

THE STIEGEL SCHOOL HOUSE, WOMELSDORF.

It is said that the Rev. John Nicholas Kurtz, of Tulpehocken, knowing the worth of the man, secured him
this position. It is known also that this once wealthy
and philanthrophic Baronial prince served as clerk, and
either with, or before, or for Mr. Ege, carried on the
Charming Forge (on the Tulpehocken) and the Reading

Furnace (now the Robesonia Furnace). The Baron
sleeps his last sleep in an unmarked grave of the Corner
(Eck) church, north of Robesonia, while Mr. Ege rests
in the Womelsdorf cemetery, with a humble stone
marking the spot.

Another old landmark is the stone house next the

THE SELTZER HOUSE, WOMELSDORF.

Lauck's mill in the eastern end of town, now occupied
and owned by Mr. Isaac S. Bechtold. It was built in
1756. Another is the Seltzer House, one of the few
hotels of the place. It is built of solid limestone, originally but two stories high, but since enlarged, and
occupies a conspicuous place along its main street at

the head of a diamond-shaped town square. It is said to be the oldest built house of the town, and claims to have lodged General Washington on one of his visits to this place. Certain it is that President Washington lodged here on the night of November 13, 1793, but two other hotels make rival claims for the honor of having furnished this shelter, viz., the Central Hotel, a public house at present kept by Mr. Isaac Y. Kintzer, and a former log hostelry known as the Middletown Hotel, occupying the lot on which now stands Mr. H. P. Fidler's handsome residence. It is quite probable that the illustrious General made several stoppages here, and that more than one of these old hotels had the honor of entertaining this distinguished guest. It is certain that in 1838 President Martin Van Buren, passing through town, breakfasted at the Seltzer House.

The town itself was laid out about 1767 by John Womelsdorf, who was either a son-in-law or grand-son-in-law of Conrad Weiser. There are old persons still living, among others Mr. and Mrs. Michael Kalbach, octogenarians and life-long residents here (she being a daughter of Peter Womelsdorf, Esq., a soldier in the war of 1812-15, and a grand-daughter of the founder of the town), who claim the former, but investigation into Conrad Weiser's family record disputes this claim and confirms the latter opinion. These aged informants recently helped the writer on the track of finding the original manuscript autobiography of Conrad Weiser, which contains most valuable historic and genealogical information, and from which a careful transcript was made. This account places the matter of John Womelsdorf marrying a daughter of Conrad Weiser in great doubt, and therefore almost settles the question of his marriage to a grand-daughter.

This being part of the Tulpehocken settlement, all its first residents worshiped either at the Reed or the other Tulpehocken churches, or else later at the Heidelberg or Eck's church, until the year 1793, when the first church of the town was erected. After this date most of the surrounding community worshiped here and buried their dead on the first graveyard here laid out. Hence, we find many of the old settlers here sleeping their last long sleep. The original walls of the Union (Lutheran and Reformed) church edifice are still standing, the building itself having undergone several remodelings. Last year the united congregations celebrated the centennial of its erection and published a brief historical sketch, from which it appears that this church was served from 1793-1809, on the Lutheran side by Rev. C. Emannel Schultze, for a few years assisted by his son, J. Andrew, afterwards Governor of the State.

Other Lutheran pastors :

Rev. Wm. Baetes 1810-1811
Rev. Daniel Ulrich 1811-1851
Rev. Thomas T. Yaeger 1851-1855
Rev. Aug. Theo. Geissenhainer 1855-1856
Rev. Lewis G. Eggers . . . . 1856- (?)

Rev. Jeff. M. Dietzler . . . . (?) –1865
Rev. Aaron Pinfrock 1865–1891
Rev. W. W. Kramlich 1892–date

The Reformed pastors were the following :

Rev. Wilhelm Hendel, D. D. 1793–1829
Rev. Frederick A Herman 1829–1834
Rev. Charles A. Pauli 1834–1855
Rev. Jacob D. Zehring 1855–1860
Rev. George Wolf, D. D. 1861–1879
Rev. David U. Wolf 1879–1881
Rev. Lewis D. Steckel 1881–1883
Rev. Levi D. Stambaugh 1884–date

Of all these pastors, the body of Dr. Hendel is the only one buried here. He sleeps near the church door by the side of his wife, suitable stones marking the spot. He was quite a power in the pulpit, and in the ranks of the Reformed ministry, in his day. The second Reformed pastor was a native of Germantown, and one of five brothers in the Reformed ministry. They were long independent of Synodical ties, but formed with others a sort of "Free Synod." To this pastor the common remark, indicative of correct preaching but somewhat inconsistent living, is traced as author, viz.: "Folget meinen Worten und nicht meinen Werken."

A stroll over the old cemetery shows us the names of old residents, long passed away, chiseled in fading epitaphs on crumbling sandstone or erasive marble, and the experience is somewhat like turning the pages of an album containing the pictures of old-time friends. Among these names are such as Fidler, Laucks, Lebenguth, Sallade, Buck, Moore, Tryon, Seibert, Kalbach, Bennethum, Schultze, Leiss, Ritschbart (Richard), Rieth (Reed), Ege, Ulrich, Stouch, Eckert, Ermentrout, Weiser, Womelsdorf, Stites, etc. We found here the graves of a few children of Governor Shulze, who at one time resided in town, and also that of his brother Frederick, for years a successful merchant of this town.

We arrange here a number of the oldest tomb-stone records, abbreviated, as it may serve some genealogical purpose some day, and be convenient for reference:

1. W. S., 1728, U. S., 1799.
2. ROBERT WOODS [M. D.], B. 1765, D. 1810.
3. JADETZ WEISER, B. 1753, D. 1829. He was blind last years of life. His wife, Marialis Weiser, a born Wengert, B. 1754, D. 1835.
4. ANNA CATHARINE SALLADE, wife of Nicholas, B. 1727, D. 1806.
5. CHRISTOFER ERMENTROUT, B. 1754, D. 1825. Also Daniel Ermentrout, B. 1798, D. 1836, and Samuel (son of Samuel and Maria Ermentrout,) B. 1835, D. 1838, and Maria Magdalena, born Moyer, wife of Johannes Ermentrout, B. 1774, D. 1846.
6. GEORGE EGE, B. 1748, D. 1829. His wife Elizabeth, born Uberfeld, B. 1746, D. 1831. Also a son, Michael Ege, and his wife, A. M. Margaret. She was a daughter of Frederick A. Shultze. Another daughter of Shultze, Harriet, was married to John Ermentrout, of Reading, whose daughter, an invalid, is deeply interested in history and genealogical lore.
7. MAGDELA RITSCHARD (Richard), a born Reber, wife of John R., B. 1765, D. 1829.
8. PETER B. ECKERT, son of Peter and Susanna E., B. 1805, D.

1824. David Eckert, son of Peter and Susanna R., B. 1795,
D. 1825.

9. FREDERICK A. SHULTZE, son of Rev. Emanuel S., B. 1777, D.
1856. Maria R. Shultze, his wife, a born Hiester. Catharine
E. Shultze, his sister, daughter of Rev. Emanuel S., B. 1782,
D. 1845. Elizabeth Shultze, daughter of (S. M.). Andreas
Shultze, B. 1802, D. 1802.

10. JACOB SELTZER, B. 1732, D. 1788.

11. ELIZABETH WEISER, daughter of Benj. and Cath. Weiser, B.
1801, D. 1803.

12. JOHN BENNETHUM, B. 1765, D 1828, and wife, Maria Barbara, a
born Minnig, and son George.

13. PETER WOMELSDORF (son of John), B. 1787, D. 1843.

14. REV. WM. HENDEL, D. D., oldest son of Rev. John William and
Elizabeth H., a born DeRoy, B. 1768, preached 50 years, D.
1846. Revs. J. C. Bucher and Thos. Leinbach officiated.

Here also is the burial place of Conrad Stouch, born
1757, died 1840, who with Calder, of Harrisburg, owned
the old-time stage line between Reading and Harrisburg, for whom Peter Kahl, of Lebanon, was a long
familiar stage driver. He used to be proprietor of the
Central Hotel.

Other old congregations of town were the Presbyterian, Universalist, New Lutheran and Evangelical, all of
which are now defunct, save the last named. The most
prominent adherents of the Universalist church were
the Longeneckers, the Manderbachs (then keeping a
hotel and summer resort at the Springs, where now the
Bethany Orphans' Home is located), the Von Neidas,
and others. Its first pastor, Rev. Mr. Longenecker, lies
buried on the Union cemetery. The church, which was

a branch of the one at Reading, never prospered, and after some years the congregation was obliged to disband. So have the other churches disbanded and merged their membership with the two or three now existing congregations.

The town enjoyed the distinction of being a far-famed business place at the end of the first quarter of this century. This was the case immediately after the opening of the Union canal, and for a decade or two afterwards it rivalled Reading itself as a business centre. Not less than ten flourishing stores were then found here, which drew their custom for many miles around. These were kept by the Moores, the Eckerts, Fred. A. Schultze, Hirsch, etc. The Ermentrouts (ancestors of the Judge of Berks county, and the other Reading Ermentrouts), and other parties here carried on a flourishing business in hat-making.

Womelsdorf has also been noted for its eminent medical men. The Tryons of several generations, and the Livingoods of at least three generations, the first of whom was a student and married the daughter of Dr. Michael Tryon (whose wife was Elizabeth Seltzer, and is buried here), the father of Drs. James C. and Louis A. Livingood, have given this town a reputation for its prominence in the medical science for a century past. Other doctors have been here to add to this reputation, such as Drs. Wood and Moore and Sallade and others.

At present, and for some time past, the chief industry here is cigar manufacturing, which has flourished in such hands as those of the well-known firms of A. S. Valentine & Son, Harry Fidler, Messrs. Balsley, Shaffner, Hackman, etc. When all these manufactories run full they employ several hundred hands, and furnish a self-sustaining revenue for these people and this town.

CHAPTER IV.

TO-DAY I mean to take you to the site of the first church built within the valley. While the Scotch-Irish of Lancaster county founded a settlement north of the South Mountain ridge early in the last century, and soon established churches at Derry, Paxtang, etc., yet there is not any doubt that the Germans, who settled along the Tulpehocken, in the eastern portion of this valley, preceded these Presbyterians in the planting of their first church, and that therefore the first church ever erected in the valley, between the Schuylkill and the Susquehanna, was the original Tulpehocken church of the Lutherans, built in 1727, now known as the Reed's church. Though this first edifice has long since given place to another, and this to a third, yet we shall visit the interesting spot and look into the remarkable life and history of this first local Christian congregation.

From Womelsdorf we can travel up the turnpike until we have crossed the bridge that spans the Tulpehocken creek and the old Union canal, just a little east of Stouchsburg, and then turn to our right, where, a quarter of a mile to the north, on a slight eminence, stands the present church, a plain stone building bear-

(38)

ing in its western wall a stone with the following inscription: "Die Zion's Kirche Erbaut im Jahr, 1837." A better and more historic highway would be to take the narrow country road that skirts the Tulpehocken, and as this is the way the first settlers traveled, we shall choose it and accompany them to church. Hence, tak-

VIEW OF THE TULPEHOCKEN.

ing the Rehrersburg road at Steigel's famous schoolhouse, and following it for half a mile to the northwest, we catch the first glimpse of the historic creek, along whose banks the events of this early settlement were enacted. Crossing this stream we turn to the left and follow the ancient road running parallel to this water-

course. The second farm-house is the old Lösch homestead, where lived an old Moravian family, by whom
the early Moravian bishops and missionaries were often
entertained while riding over this circuit. The house
was erected by Johannes Jacob Lösch in 1754, and his
son or brother, George, was a leader in the Hebron
Moravian church for many years.

THE LÖSCH HOMESTEAD.

A little farther up the road is the Reed homestead,
which remains substantially the same internally as when
erected in 1723, by Loenhardt Rieth, the donor of the
eight acres of ground upon which the church was built in
1727. The seventh lineal descendant, Mr. Franklin B.
Reed still occupies this ancient homestead, and has gath-

ered into it many valuable local church documents, some family bric-a-brac, and a large collection of Indian relics.

A short distance from this latter house stands the old Reed Church. Its location on a small knoll is alluded

THE REED HOMESTEAD.

to in the following lines, from the pen of Mr. L. A. Wollenweber:

"Do droben uf dem runde Berg,
Do steht die alte Riethe-Kerch;
Drin hot der Parre Stoever schon
Vor hunnert Jahr manch Predigt thun;
Gepredigt zu de arme, deitsche Leit
In seller, ach! so harten Zeit.

4

Auch wor die Kerch'u gute Fort
Gegen der Indianer wilde Hort—
Un schliefen drin gar manche Nacht,
Die arme Settlers wo hen bewacht."

FIRST TULPEHOCKEN (REEL.) LUTHERAN CHURCH.

The history of the erection of this first church, and
the checkered story of its congregational life, to the
present time is very interesting. It was in 1723 that
about 60 families of German Lutherans immigrated

hither from the Schoharie Valley of New York, where they had taken up a temporary abode in their flight from French Jesuitical persecutions in the Fatherland. Queen Anne of England proved to them a benefactress in sheltering them first of all in London, and then gratuitously transporting them to these new colonies of her realm. But the English money sharks up the Hudson took the advantage of these innocent Germans, and soon beat them out of their possessions, when many of them came to this Tulpehocken country, and once more planted their humble huts in the wild forests among the Indians. They reached these parts by following the Susquehanna, until they came to the mouth of the Swatara creek, where now is situated Middletown; thence up this latter creek and across the divide, where they found this rich valley along the Tulpehocken. They were followed in 1729 by another exodus from Schoharie, among whom was Conrad Weiser and his family.

But scarcely had the first party arrived, and built for themselves humble sheltering homes, when they contemplated the erection of a house of worship. Accordingly a public meeting was called in 1727, to which they invited all the settlers in a circumference of twenty miles. This convention was held in a log house or Indian fort, standing on the banks of the Millcreek, near Newmanstown, which fort had been erected for protection and defence against the Indians. It gave place in 1745 to a stone-fort still standing, and to which I propose to lead my readers in a later excursion.

At this called meeting the widely scattered German settlers were well represented. It is generally supposed that there was present also the Rev. Johann Casper Stoever, who afterward resided at Conestoga, Lancaster county, and in 1737 took up his abode in what is now Lebanon county, (two miles west of Lebanon, along the Quittapahilla), and lies buried at the Hill church on Lebanon county soil. But that statement is a mistake, for he did not land at Philadelphia from the Fatherland until September 11, 1728, or over a year after the above event. He did, however, soon after his arrival, become intimately associated with this church enterprise. But the erection of this first house of worship was wholly the work of the laity, and the credit belongs to such pious leaders among them as the Reith (Reed) brethren, Adam and Leonhardt, the former of whom is said to have presided at this meeting, and the latter to have donated sufficient land for church, school-house and burial purposes, over eight acres in all. One George Scholl is said to have made the motion to erect a house of worship, which was unanimously carried. Other leading lights in this convention were Michael Reith, Frederick and Michael Schaeffer, and Christopher Lechner, upon whom fell the choice of the superintendence of the erection of the building. It is asserted that in the devotions conducted at this meeting, Luther's famous battle-hymn "Ein Feste Burg," was sung. If it was not as well rendered as it was at the "Luther Entertainment" at the Fisher opera house recently by the hundred of Miss Munshower's trained singers, it must have been equally appropriate and just as thrilling.

Under Mr. Lechner's superintendence, and by the assistance of men and women helpers, this first Tulpehocken church was completed in five months and dedicated in October of the same year (1727). It is not likely that any pastor was present at this dedication service, though it is generally claimed that Rev. Stoever officiated. If this, indeed, be true, then the church was not consecrated until a year after its completion. But as the parochial teacher stood next to the minister in official rank in those days, and as we know one was long employed to conduct religious worship in absence of a pastor, and that the parochial school was established here from the beginning, it is possible that the first teacher, whose name was Jacob Hanumer, a native of Manheim, Germany, officiated at the dedication of this first church.

The building consisted of hewn logs, with roof of thatch or tiles. The pews were made of the same material (logs with a hewn side for seats), while the pulpit was made of rough boards. An ordinary walnut table, 34x48 inches in dimensions, donated by one of the Reiths, was used as altar and communion table, which identical table is still intact, the property of Aaron Snyder, Esq., a lineal descendant of donor, living at Mt. Ætna, Berks county, Pa.—a relic of 167 years.

The question of employing a regularly ordained Lutheran minister as pastor became the most puzzling problem to these early worshipers. There were then but very few German Lutheran pastors in the entire country, and probably not a single one within the limits of the State, as J. Casper Stoever is said to have been the first *German* Lutheran pastor in Pennsylvania. A few Swedish and Dutch pastors had preceded him. So these people had to be content with lay preaching, and were thus liable to be often imposed upon. Now the Moravians, in the name and garb of Lutheran pastors, supplied their spiritual wants; now a parochial teacher, falsely claiming to have been ordained, assumed the office of the minister, until the congregation was thus thrown into almost hopeless confusion and into different factions. The troubles continued for a period of 10 or 12 years, in which it was necessary to call in the officers of the law and the advice of church authorities in the Fatherland, and the German court preacher at London, Dr. Ziegenhagen. This dispute is described minutely in the "Halle Reports" (*Hallischen Nachrichten*)— being the preserved correspondence of these early Lutherans with the mission school at Halle, Germany.

The nearest justice of the peace was Wm. Webb, of Kennett, Chester county, who was lawful attorney for John Page, of London, the proprietor of these Tulpehocken lands under the title of the Manor of Plumpton. A document drawn up by this Mr. Webb, giving exclusive rights to church property to the Leibbecker party—one of the factions of this early dispute—and bearing date of January 22, 1735, is still kept as a relic by Mr. Franklin B. Reed, the seventh lineal descendant of the Leonhardt Reith who donated the church grounds, and whose old homestead, a quarter of a mile east of the church, we have described. Upon the death of Leibbecker, teacher and pastor, the Moravians made their appearance and offered to supply the pulpit without remuneration. Thus through Count Zinzendorf's supervision pastors of his appointment preached to one party of Lutherans for about eight years. But though these claimed to be Lutherans, it only widened the breach within the congregation, and led in 1742 to the founding of a new church, purely Lutheran, which erected its building about a mile west of the former edifice, and named itself Christ Lutheran church. This church, now generally known as the Tulpehocken Lutheran church, has prospered very much more than the first from its very beginning, and will form the subject of our next sketch.

Reed's church was brought back to the Lutheran fold through the influence of Conrad Weiser and his son-in-law, Henry Melchoir Muhlenberg, in September, 1747, and has remained loyal to its first foundation ever since. The pastors who have served it since that time are Rev. J. Nicholas Kurtz, 1748–1770; Rev. Christopher E. Schultze, 1770–1809; Rev. Daniel Ulrich, 1811–1851; Rev. L. G. Eggers, 1852–1853; Rev. Thomas T. Jaeger, 1853–1865; Rev. Aaron Finfrock, 1865–1886; Rev. E. S. Brownmiller, 1886–date.

In the graveyard adjoining this ancient church are many old graves and quaintly engraved tombstones. It is well worth a visit to see the first Macpelah of these devout pioneers. The lessons one can learn of primitive art, orthography and genealogy, as he passes from one crumbling and moss-covered sandstone to another, will repay him for his trouble. Though they be but humble monuments, almost every old stone marks the resting-place of a hero, who has faced persecution, exile, poverty, and the cruel barbarisms of the red-man. We will give the inscriptions—minus the quaint art embellishments—of but two in closing this chapter. The one is that of the donor of the land—the other that one of Conrad Weiser's sons. They read as follows:

1747

HR LIGD BE-
GRABEN OHAN
LOENHARD RITH
BR IST GEBOHREN
1691 VND GESTORBEN
1747
ER HAT MIT SEINER
HAVS FRAV ANA
LISA CATHARINA
GEZEVGT 8 KINDER
65 OENKELEIN

Engraved on both sides:

UND IN

SOLCHER ZEIT

ERZEVGTE ER KIN-

DER ALS 3 SOEHNE

UND 1 TOCHTERLEIN

OVON DAS

TOCHTERLEIN WIE-

DER GESTORBEN

UND 3 SOEHNE

SIND NOCH AM

LEBEN

DIESES

IST DIE RUHE

STATTE DES WEYLAND

EHRSAMEN PHILIP

WEISERS. DERSELBE WARE

GEBOHREN IM IAHR

1722

DEN 7 SEPTEMBER UND

GESTORBEN ANNO

1761

dEN 27 MERTZ SEI-

NES ALTERS 38 IAHR

5 MONAT VND 4

TAG VND HATTE IN DER EHR

GELEBET 12 IAHR 4 MONAT

U

CHAPTER V.

We noticed in the last chapter that in consequence of the division and confusion of the original Tulpehocken congregation in its early history, a very large portion of the same withdrew in 1743, and erected a church of their own. We will to-day follow these seceders to the spot they then chose upon which to build their new church, and, while walking over these historic and sacred grounds, take a peep into the history of 150 years of local church-life.

The faction withdrawing from Reed's church was by far the stronger of the two in numbers and influence. Though deprived of the use of the church edifice by the legal document alluded to in our last, they were the pure Lutherans in doctrine and practice, and were contending at that early period of American Lutheranism for the *Reine Lehre* of their ecclesiastical faith.

Accordingly they were willing to make sacrifices and begin anew the building of a church and the development of true religion as confessed by their Church. There was, therefore, drawn up a document setting forth the principles upon which this new church should be founded—which carefully guards against their admixture with any sects and errorists, by whom they had

(50)

formerly been deceived. The same was signed by 166 adherents, and the original copy placed in the corner-stone of the church, which was laid in May, 1743.

TULPEHOCKEN (CHRIST) LUTHERAN CHURCH AND CEMETERY.

Another copy of the same paper has ever since been carefully kept with the church archives, and was trans-lated into English and embodied, together with the names of the signers, in an historical address by the

Rev. F. J. F. Schantz, of Myerstown, which address was delivered at the sesqui-centennial services held last September. We trust this very important address may some day be given the public in pamphlet form.* This second Tulpehocken church received the name of Christ Lutheran church, but has for years been known as the Tulpehocken Lutheran church. It stands about a mile west of the Reed church, just outside the western limits of Stouchsburg, and a few hundred yards south of the Berks and Dauphin turnpike. The original building, which was probably of logs, and the foundation stones of which can still be seen, was replaced by a second one in 1786. This structure was of stone, and is still standing, a venerable pile of solid masonry. Parts of the building have been renewed and remodeled, but the walls remain intact, and bid fair to defy the ravages of time and the elements for another hundred years and more. The building was dreadfully shaken up by a dynamite explosion which occurred in the vicinity November 6, 1884, and had all its woodwork destroyed by fire, caused by lightning, August 1, 1887, yet the original walls are as solid, and stand as plumb, as when they were first finished. At its last remodeling, in 1887, a marble slab was placed in its western side, showing to all visitors the following engraved record of pastorates:

---

*It has since been so published.

PASTORS OF CHRIST'S TULPEHOCKEN LUTHERAN CHURCH.

Rev. Tobias Wagner, 1743-1746.
Rev. John Nicholas Kurtz, 1748-1770.
Rev. Christopher Emanuel Schultze, 1770-1809.
Rev. Daniel Ulrich, 1811-1851.
Rev. Louis E. Eggers, 1852-1867.
Rev. Frederick P. Mayser, 1868-1873.
Rev. A. Johnson Long, 1874-

The time and place of the decease of such pastors, as have died, are appended to the above record.

The interior of the church is modern in style and convenient in arrangement. With a basement for Sunday-school purposes, and an audience room on the second floor surrounded by a half-moon gallery, the church within is a thing of beauty as a rural edifice. Here worship regularly several hundred of the sturdy descendants of an even sturdier ancestry.

Here have preached some of the most scholarly and eloquent ministers of the Lutheran church. Pastor Kurtz was a godly man, and a power in his day. From him have descended the family of Kurtzes, who in the ministry and the laity have been famous for a century in this branch of the American church. And seldom has a congregation the privilege of enjoying such intellectually strong and spiritual pastoral services as were rendered during the two long-continued pastorates of Revs. Schultze and Ulrich, the former the father of ex-Governor John Andreas Schultze, (now Shulze) of Pennsylvania, and the latter the father of a highly respected progeny still largely represented in this com-

TULPEHOCKEN LUTHERAN GRAVEYARD.

munity and throughout this valley. The bodies of both
these godly men sleep within the old graveyard adjoining. The epitaph of the former reads as follows:

Hier Ruhet
Christoph Immanuel
Schultze, Prediger.
war geboren den
25 December 1740
Saatfeld in Sachsen.
Er kam in das
Abend land 1765
Im Ehestand lebte
Er mit seiner Ehefrau
Eva Elizabeth 43 Jahr
Als Prediger staud er
5 Jahr in Philadelphia
und 38 Jahr in Tulpehocken,
Hinterlies 9 Kinder
und starb den 11 Martz 1809
Alt 68 Jahr, 2 Monat 2 Wochen

By the side of Pastor Schultze sleeps his wife, who was a daughter of Rev. Henry Melchoir Muhlenberg, the Lutheran Patriarch, and a grand-daughter of Conrad Weiser, and the mother of Gov. Schultze.

The epitaph of Rev. Ulrich is in English, and reads as follows:

In
Memory of
REV. DANIEL ULRICH,
Born
near Annville, Lebanon Co., Pa., Aug.
10, 1789.
He early dedicated his life to his God, and entered the ministry in 1809. He became the pastor of the United congregations of Tulpehocken, Rehrersburg, Heidelberg and others, whom he faithfully served from the year 1811, to the year 1851.
Died June 2nd, 1855, while on a visit to Pittsburg, Pa.
Aged 65 y. 9 m, and 22 days.

The ancient cemetery contains many other old graves, which must have a meaning to the descendants, in many instances famous to-day in Church or State. We will mention but a few. For instance, the writer was astonished to find here the graves of Philip Breitenbach and his wife Elizabeth, evidently the ancestors of the family by that name at Gettysburg, who in a pastoral or

professional capacity have served the Church for years.
Here also lived and are buried the first and second
generations of the ancestry (on the mother's side) of our
U. S. Senator, Hon. J. Donald Cameron. The Senator's
mother—wife of the late Hon. Simon Cameron—was a
Brua, a Lutheran in faith, and a daughter of Peter
Brua, who as a lay delegate from Tulpehocken helped
to organize the General Synod of the Lutheran Church
in 1820, and whose father, Peter Brua, was one of the
early German settlers at Tulpehocken. His grave and
that of his wife are side by side in this graveyard, and
the inscriptions on their tomb-stones read as follows:

Hier Ruhet	Hier Ruhet
Peter Brua	Maria Brua
war gebohren	Ehefrau von
den 2 Feber 1729	Peter Brua
und starb	Gebohren
den 1 October 1808	1731
war alt	Gestorben
79 Jahre 8 Monat	1804
	73 Jahre 6 Monat

But the spot in this city of last century's dead that
holds the most charm for the visitor, if indeed a graveyard can have charms, is that which, though unmarked
by memorial stones, is pointed out as the resting place
of the famed Hartman family, so cruelly murdered by
the Indians, and whose captive daughter, Regina, and

her surviving mother, form the principal characters in Rev. Dr. Reuben Weiser's interesting book, entitled "Regina, the German Captive." It is said that Regina herself sleeps here her last long sleep, and the spot of earth covering her dust is pointed out by the sexton, though not a marker is there to help the visitor, unattended by one who knows, to find the place. Let us now turn away from these sacred surroundings, with their hallowed and historic associations, deferring, until the next chapter, a sketch of our visit to the more than interesting parsonage that stands within the shadow of this church.

5

CHAPTER VI.

AN INTERESTING OLD MANSE.

WE shall to-day visit the Tulpehocken Lutheran parsonage. And standing upon the threshold of this antiquated ministerial abode, I shall ask my fellow-explorers to step lightly and reverently on entering a door that has

THE TULPEHOCKEN LUTHERAN PARSONAGE.

swung on its hinges for one hundred and fifty years to give entrance and exit, not only to the long line of its

(58)

pious and honored inmates, but to hundreds, yea thousands, besides. In addition to the usual social and parish visits made here in its long history, this is the door that has opened to many a hundred couple of young lovers who came hither to have nuptial knots tied by the dominie in charge. Here many another hundred calls were made to announce the death of some parishioner and engage the pastor's services for the funeral. Hither many an infant was borne by loving parents—though probably more to the church itself—to have the rite of holy baptism administered. While not all these official acts may have been performed in the parsonage, it appears from an historical address delivered by Rev. Schantz at the sesqui-centennial celebration of the church, that there are records preserved showing that for a part of this period, covering a very large parish, the various pastors residing here officiated at 6,934 baptisms, 3,829 marriages, and 2,518 funerals. Of course the record is incomplete in every one item, as for periods of years together one or the other class of entries was discontinued.

Beyond a doubt, the most interesting wedding that ever occurred here was that of the Rev. Henry Melchoir Muhlenberg, the eminent patriarch of the Lutheran Church in America, then resident in Philadelphia, to Miss Annie Marie Weiser, a daughter of the celebrated Conrad Weiser. It was solemnized by the first pastor, Rev. Tobias Wagner, in 1745, and forms a most conspicuous entry in the intensely interesting Church Record begun by him, and still preserved and continued. If, indeed, this illustrious pair were not married in this identical house, which seems to have been built a year or two later, it was yet solemnized on this spot, in a house adjoining, which as a part of a mill property, was then used as the pastor's residence, and which is still standing and in possession of the congregation.

A book of accounts is kept at the parsonage to this day, as one of the congregation's most valuable historic relics, showing, in Pastor Kurtz's handwriting, an account of receipts and expenditures in pounds, shillings and pence, contributed and disbursed during the building of this house. The erection of this building occurred during the first years of this pastor's official service here. He was called in 1746, and served as catechist until 1748, when at the first meeting of the oldest Synod of the Lutheran Church in America (the Ministerium of Pennsylvania and Adjacent States), convened in St. Michael's Church of Philadelphia, he was ordained as the first American Lutheran minister so set apart by order and act of an organized ecclesiastical body. It was, therefore, in the newly completed and occupied parsonage that he prepared himself for this Synodic examination. Whatever stress may have been laid by this young candidate for the ministry in his previous study upon purely theological points, the following practical questions were some that were laid before him for answer, by the Committee, viz.: *What are the evidences of conversion? What is meant by the* *influence and blessings of the Holy Spirit? How do you prove that Christ was not only a teacher, but that He made an atonement for the sins of man?* etc. At his ordination, Rev. Hartwig preached from the words, "His blood will I require at thy hand." It may have been some impression made upon his mind by this sermon, that made this pastor of Tulpehocken such a faithful and earnest preacher and worker for souls. In all these perilous years (when in his home or on his journeys he was constantly exposing his life to danger from the attacks of the Indians, who frequently invaded the territory of his parish and tomahawked or scalped entire families, many of whom he was called upon to bury *) he kept faithfully at his post, never neglecting his work as pastor and preacher.

It was while residing in this parsonage that his large family of children were born, consisting of nine sons and three daughters. The baptism of at least eight of them is recorded in the Church Record kept here. One of these is that of John Daniel, who himself became an eminent minister, and spent a few years of his life as assistant to his father, then residing at York, and later as assistant pastor to, and soon as successor of Rev. Goerock, of Baltimore. He was pastor of the first Lutheran church of that city for 46 years, when he retired, living

* In a letter to Dr. Muhlenberg, in 1757, he says, that "on one day not less than seven members of the congregation were brought to the church for burial, having been murdered by the Indians the day before."

to the extraordinary age of 93. He at one time refused a call from Salem Lutheran church of Lebanon.

Another son of pastor John Nicholas Kurtz, of Tulpehocken, was long the parochial teacher of the York Lutherans. He was the father of the Rev. Dr. Benj. Kurtz—one of the most eminent men the Lutheran Church of America ever produced, who as preacher, author, editor of the *Lutheran Observer*, and one of the chief founders of the institutions of classical and theological learning at Gettysburg and Selinsgrove, and of the Evangelical Alliance, and as traveller abroad, has acquired a reputation as wide as the Church.

A daughter of this Tulpehocken Pastor Kurtz, and born in this manse, afterwards became the wife of Rev. Jacob Goering, of York, concerning whom a church historian said, at the time of his death, "many generations must pass away before the world will look upon his equal." Through the marriage of a grand-daughter (the daughter of Rev. John Daniel Kurtz) this family also became connected with that of the gifted Lutheran divines, the Schaeffers, and their two children became famous, the one being Rev. Dr. Charles F. Schaeffer, long a professor at the Theological Seminary at Gettysburg, and the other the wife of the Rev. Dr. Demme, of Philadelphia, one of the most learned men of this century.

We see, therefore, what a celebrated progeny came from the family which occupied this parsonage for the first twenty years after its erection.

That Pastor Kurtz, the senior, was himself a man of eminent literary attainments, is inferred by the respect accorded him by so renowned a literary institution as the College of New Jersey, whose Faculty regularly sent him special invitations to attend their annual Commencements, though Tulpehocken was considerably distant from Princeton.

But other prominent families succeeded that of Pastor Kurtz as occupants of this manse. His immediate successor was Rev. Christoph Emanuel Schultze, for several years previous the assistant pastor to Dr. H. M. Muhlenberg, of Philadelphia. He was a native of Saxony, Germany, and a graduate of the institutions at Halle. He arrived in this country in 1765 newly ordained to the ministry, and as associate of Dr. Muhlenberg served both the St. Michael's and Zion's churches of Philadelphia. The latter was founded during his ministry there, and was, at the time, regarded as the handsomest church edifice in this country. It was to this church that Congress repaired in a body to express thanksgiving to God for the victory of the Revolutionary army and the restoration of peace on the surrender of Cornwallis at Yorktown. The same edifice had also been used as a hospital by the British during their occupancy of Philadelphia. But Pastor Schultze had left Philadelphia long before this occurred, although he was strongly urged by this flock to return. He took up his abode at Tulpehocken in 1770, having previously married Eva Elizabeth, daughter of Patriarch Muhlenberg. Here he labored, occupying this mause, for thirty-eight years, with the house again, as in the case of Pastor Kurtz, filling up with children. There were niue children in all, of whom the most conspicuous was John Andrew, born here, who, after a short ministerial career, entered secular life and served this State for two terms as Governor. His administration is still conspicuously remembered for its justice and intelligence; and Lebanon enjoys the proud distinction of having numbered him as one of her residents when his fellow citizens of the State elevated him to this high office.

The many arduous and fatiguing labors of Pastor Schultze so enfeebled his body, that during the last year of his life he had often to be assisted to the pulpit. The Sunday preceding his death he was too weak to leave the house, so he summoned the congregation to the parsonage, where he preached his last sermon. The following Saturday, March 11, 1809, he fell asleep in Christ, following his lamented wife, who had a few months previously preceded him to the bosom of a loving Saviour. Rev. Dr. Lochman, of Lebanon, preached his funeral sermon the following Wednesday, from the words: "If any man serve me, let him follow me; and where I am, there shall also my servant be." A portion of Pastor Schultze's valuable library was afterwards presented to Pennsylvania College.

All the successors in this historic parsonage have helped to make the abode famous by long residence and noble deeds. Here the well-remembered Rev. Daniel

Ulrich, a native of Lebanon county, resided for forty years. He was followed by the families of Parsons Eggers, Mayser and Long, the last of whom is now the genial occupant, who, with his accomplished wife, has in training a small family of children, whose noble deeds, we trust, will keep up the good repute this abode has gained by the high character of those who have dwelt here or gone out from hence.

CHAPTER VII.

To-day we shall turn away from the pious and peaceful scenes of churches, graveyards and parsonages, and visit a relic that speaks to us of the perils and trials of Indian warfare. It is well worth our study to know what our forefathers endured in those early days in consequence of their treacherous and oft barbaric neighbors —the red-skinned savages. For this purpose let the mute monuments of heroic defense and protection, still found here and there throughout our valley in the shape of strongly-built Indian forts, be our teachers. We turn away, therefore, from the long-honored and historic abode of five generations of preachers to one of the best preserved houses of refuge and defense against these savage hordes. As this is still keeping its vigil in this valley, and is close at hand, let me lead the way to it.

Striking right across the country from Stouchsburg to the south, past Sheridan station on the Lebanon Valley railroad, we keep on the Mill Creek road, due south, for another half mile, when we come to the Zeller homestead, and here we find, on the banks of the Mill Creek, this interesting relic of those ancient and trying times. It is commonly known as the Zeller Indian fort, because

(66)

originally built by a Zeller, and since the land, upon which it was erected, is claimed never to have gone out of Zeller hands to the present time.

The fort is a well-sized and well-proportioned stone structure, a story and a half high, built with a capacious cellar, half under ground, from which flows a strong and beautiful stream of clear water, having its rise here

ZELLER INDIAN FORT, BUILT IN 1745.

in a perennial spring. It was erected by Heinrich Zeller, in 1745, as is shown from an engraved headstone within the wall. It is kept in good repair, used mostly for a farmer's storage house at present, but until the present generation had long been occupied as a weaver's shop. About fifty feet away, the place is pointed out where Heinrich Zeller, in 1723, built the first house of logs, which it is claimed was the first meeting place of those early Schoharie settlers for worship and defence and mutual conference. Here it was where action was taken to erect the first house of worship in 1727, which led to the erection of the original Tulpehocken Church, already described. This house was displaced, in 1745, by the stone fort in question. The name of Henry 'Zeller frequently occurs in the Colonial Records of that day, principally in connection with correspondence concerning the title to his lands. It seems there was considerable difficulty in gaining a good title, as we find it was 1743, or twenty years after settlement here, that he obtained legal papers. These documents are parchment deeds, or land patents, bearing the signature of the Penn heirs, John, Thomas and Richard Penn, and are still preserved among the family archives.

Thus this permanent building was not erected until a good deed had been secured for the land upon which this original settler had squatted, and which he had meanwhile improved, and possibly later satisfactorily paid for to the proper owners.

The occasion for building the house in the form of a citadel, or refuge fortification, was constantly at hand. Many were the cruel depredations of the red men in that period. Frequently the Indian war-whoop was heard, and the tomahawk and scalping-knife were flourished by these savage foes. Many an unwary white traveler or tiller of the soil was dispatched, and frequently whole families were scalped and butchered. These houses of refuge were therefore erected in different parts of the settlement, to afford the settlers of each locality a safe rendezvous, whither the community could flee for safety at the first signal of peril. Thus we find a considerable number of buildings still standing throughout our valley that were used for this purpose. This one was among the first to be erected, and most centrally situated for the earliest settlement.

The building itself is a curiosity. Its walls are two feet thick, and laid up with many large and well-dressed stones. Its door-posts, about five and a half feet high, and the lintel, fully three feet long, are single sandstones, with some attempts at carved ornamentation upon them. The head-stone over the door, and the slab bearing name and date, have rather elaborate figures and lines carved upon them. The door is broken into two, like ordinary stable doors, and consists of double inch boards pegged together with wooden pins. An iron catch, or staple, on the inside, soldered with lead into the stone door-post, catches the heavy iron latch that closes the door. All the windows were originally but small square port-holes in the wall; but three of these have since been enlarged into the size of ordinary windows, for the accommodation of the cloth weaver who plied his craft here a generation or two ago. The rest remain intact. So does the building throughout. Its main floor, over the cellar, is arched below and leveled with stone and earth. A huge and quaint Queen Anne fireplace, twelve feet wide, graces the kitchen part of the house. In the wall, forming the chimney, is a crack or mark, which tradition says

was made by a cannon ball shot through one of the
port-holes during the Colonial struggles with the
French and Indians. The writer has seen both the
break in the wall and the cannon ball, which is preserved here, but he is not prepared to authenticate the
story. It is an historical fact, however, that in 1755
these hostile forces crossed the Susquehanna from the
west, and invaded this eastern territory. It was at this
time when Col. Conrad Weiser wrote his rousing letters to the proprietary Quaker government of the State,
with headquarters at Philadelphia, urging speedy efforts
at defense of its citizens. At the same time he himself
summoned together the farmers of this community, and
at this very house (if, indeed, the claim made by a certain writer be correct, that this was then the residence
of Benjamin Spycher, which, however, is gravely
doubtful,) organized a company of over three hundred
men, who, after summoning Pastor Kurtz to address
them and offer a prayer in their behalf, marched up the
valley towards the Susquehanna, with their weapons of
pitchforks and flintlocks, to repel the foe.

An interesting story is told, on what seems reliable
traditionary evidence, of how the heroic wife of Heinrich Zeller, Christine by name, one day, while all alone
in the house, decapitated, with a broad-ax, three prowling and plundering Indians at the cellar loop-hole.
This hole is on the side on which the water flows out
from the spring within, and is shown in the foregoing
cut. Seeing the plunderers stealthily approach this

spot, sneaking up the little streamlet, she is said to have quickly descended the cellar 'steps from within, and stationed herself alongside this opening with weapon upraised. Presently the head of the first Indian protruded through the hole, when down came her weapon with a heavy blow. It had its desired effect. Promptly dragging the trunk through the hole, she, in a disguised Indian tongue, gave notice for the other two to follow, as all was right within. Presently the second victim followed, whom she dispatched in the same bloody manner—likewise the third; glorying on the return of her husband at night, like Deborah of old over her conquest of their treacherous Gentile foes.

The Zeller homestead, consisting of a farm of over 200 acres of rich land, upon which are erected a large and inviting stone mansion and all the necessary farmbuildings in proper proportions and style, near which this ancient fort is keeping its watch, is now the property of Mr. Monroe P. Zeller, the eighth lineal descendant of the original Heinrich. He is a brother-in-law of Rev. Bachman, the Reformed minister of Schaefferstown. He is himself talented and cultured. A graduate of Franklin and Marshall college and of several musical conservatories, he made a small fortune in giving instructions in music in Louisville, Ky., with which money he has purchased and improved the old home. He has travelled abroad and brought with him vines and shrubbery from many an interesting shrine or locality of Great Britain, Germany and Scandinavia.

When the writer first visited the place, a few years ago,
the spacious yard abounded with evergreens and choice
vines from different countries of Europe, while the east
end of the "fort" itself was spun over with a luxurious
growth of Scotch ivy, brought directly from Holyrood
Castle. The old homestead has many charms, and is
well worth a visit some summer day, by any one in love
with nature, art or history.

CHAPTER VIII.

AN ANTIQUATED VILLAGE.

IF my readers will follow me one-half mile to the southeast, from the Indian fort last visited, I will bring them to one of the oldest villages in the valley. In appearance it has perhaps changed least of any of the first *dorfs* reared by these early settlers. It is the village of Newmanstown, situated in the northeast corner of Millcreek township, Lebanon county, and at the intersection of the Schaefferstown and Womelsdorf road with the Sheridan and Lancaster county road, which leads through the South Mountain gap or pass. It formed an early trade and home center for the first settlers of this community. Let us together take a walk through its one long street.

There is nothing to indicate that its first land-owner and founder was not a full-blooded German except its name. We feel confident that were some weary traveler of Germany, some scissors-grinder or Jewish peddler or other tramp, to fall asleep some night after a day's weary march from village to village in one of the rustic hamlets in the heart of Germany, and during his slumbers be transferred to the village now in question and awaken here, he would scarcely discover that he was

(73)

not in Germany still, so genuinely *Fatherlandish* is
everything in the architecture and manners of this
well-preserved hamlet of a century and a half ago.
We will not have gone a dozen yards in our ramble
before pictures of German village life, as it existed at
the beginning of the last century, impress themselves
upon our view on every hand. We will discover that
whatever specimens of foreign village scenes were
shown the visitors of Midway Plaisance at the World's
Fair last year, the best type of a German village is
found here at Newmanstown. The street is wide and
well graded, but the pavements have received little
attention. There may be attempts at paving here and
there by the use of irregular pieces of flagging or
patches of coppery-greenish brick walks, but generally
the spaces before the little one-storied huts are covered
over with grass, while narrow, well-beaten footpaths
lead through the same. Curbstones are generally missing. One is obliged to make sudden rises and descents
in walking along, like unto the varying cadences in
music, so uneven is the grading. Fully half the houses
along its main street, which is "close unto a mile" in
length, are the originally low, one-storied log cabins,
some receiving more recently tight-fitting bodices of
weather-boards. Our city (Lebanon) has specimens of
these early dwellings in the older portions of Chestnut
and Walnut streets, and a few excellent types on North
Sixth street. Some of these Newmanstown homes still
wear their original covers of straw or tiling, their roofs

so low that the pedestrian sauntering along might almost touch the eaves. One of these houses may be on a slight elevation of ground, while its next door neighbor seems to be anxious to hide itself in its own cellar. The needful but unexpected slopes or steps that accommodate the saunterer on its streets to these rises and deflections are what are doing the mischief to his unaccustomed feet, leading the strange wayfarer into many a stumble or misstep.

The wiser way of getting along here is to follow the custom of its own citizens and exchange pavement for street. And this we will do. It may result in making us a trifle more conspicuous, but then the chances are we will be stared at nevertheless, not for any novelty in this respect, but because of our own expressions of surprise and wonderment, and because the windows of these one or two-roomed huts have been made to front on the street and to look out by. But this walk through the middle of the street will bring us right to the antiquated well, found in the central spot, where for a century and a half these pleasant villagers have been drawing their water. It is a pity that the old sweep has been exchanged for the more modern pump-handle with which to bring up the cooling draught. That would complete the picture of rusticity and antiquity. For the cackling goose, and the village gossip, and the cow or horse watering at its trough, are seldom missing to give the picture reality.

Along this street we see among these first dwellings

and their more modern and pretentious neighbors now
studding the village on every hand, the old-time artisan
shops, in line with these homes and fronting on the
street. Here half a dozen generations of honest and
busy mechanics have plied their honest crafts and eked
out an humble living. The lively ring of the tempered
steel upon the anvil gives notice that we are approaching a brawny smith's establishment. The leather chips
on the sidewalk betray that we have reached a cobbler's
or saddler's headquarters, while another window may
give us a glimpse of the tailor, as he sits cross-legged on
his table. So we will pass the lock or gunsmith shop,
the broom-maker's shanty, the cooper's establishment,
the turner's, weaver's or tinner's workshop or ware-
room—likewise the factory of that more modern crafts-
man, the cigar-maker. But here all trades are upon the
same level—the level of the street; and all craftsmen
put on the same bold front—the frontage on the street.
Even a few offensive barnyards have not in these 150
years been relegated, by this simple peasantry, whither
they deserved to be put, on the back of the lot, or
"into innocuous desuetude."

As we pass along we see here an octogenarian on his
portico, resting the weight of his body and years upon
his tottering cane. Now we pass a rosy-faced matron
down on her knees at the front stoop, scrubbing the
door-step with a determination as if the salvation of her
soul depended upon it. Perhaps it does. At least she
does not allow any externals to interfere with her task

of working it out with a good deal of shaking, if not of fear and trembling. Now the cripple upon his crutch passes us, and then that ubiquitous unfortunate of every old town, the demented, meets our eye, whose vacant stare and incoherent utterances tell the character, if not the story, of his affliction. The dogs recognize us as strangers, and vociferously chide us for our mental criticism of their goodly province.

Having finally completed our stroll, I must take time to tell you of the village's history, and give you an account of its more modern improvements. Instead of being founded by a German, it was an Irish immigrant who first planted his home here, and, securing possession of the land, began to lay it out in village building lots. This person was a Mr. Walter Newman, who purchased of the proprietors of the Province of Pennsylvania, October 30, 1741, a tract of 234 acres of land. Lots were at once sold on the "ground rent" plan, and the earliest name given the village was *Newbury*. Indentures are still on record which describe the lots disposed of, and on what terms sales were made at that early day. Much of this tract remained, by transfer from father to son, in the Newman family unto the end of the last century, by which time "Newman's Town" is described by a certain Lancaster document as being "on the Great Road leading to Reading." To this very day almost the entire town is under the curse of that system of taxation, adopted and made forever obligatory by its founder, of leasing lots for the consideration of a yearly rent. Even a large portion of the surrounding country was for some time under this feudal system.

Let no one imagine, however, from the foregoing account, that the inhabitants of this ancient hamlet are fossilized. Although there are many antiquated relics in the shape of dwellings, yet there have been rising up during the last decades many lovely and imposing structures, used as homes or business places. The streets leading out of it in every direction are models for grading, piking and good-keeping generally. There is much less mud there in a square mile of roadway than in one block of Lebanon's highways. Nor does the old pump any longer serve as chief supply to the villagers of the crystal beverage, inasmuch as a few years since the coldest and clearest of mountain water was introduced from the Gold Springs of the South Mountain "Kluft." It is said when the trenches were dug to lay the main pipe of this water supply that a rare old relic was found imbedded in the earth. This was a clay or stone Indian pipe, in the shape of a tomahawk, bearing the name of William Penn upon its bowl. I cannot vouch for the correctness of the rumor, but heard it at the time it was said to have been found, and from men of the community. Neither could I give any relic-hunter direction as to where this rare specimen is now kept.

Nor has this village failed to furnish its due quota of progressive and useful men. From its citizens have

come a number of men who have graced all the learned
professions and nobler walks of life.   Perhaps the most
conspicuous illustration of this truth, however, was in
the person of Prof. Lawrence J. Ibach, but recently
deceased.   A native of Allentown, Pa., he moved hither
with his parents at the age of 19.   He was by trade a

STREET SCENE IN NEWMANSTOWN, PA.

skillet and ladle-maker, which trade he here followed,
and never wholly forsook to the day of his death, though
higher honors and more important labors were heaped
upon him.   Through business relations with a Mr.
Seidle, from whom he had for a few years rented a forge
near Reading, he became acquainted with the latter's

uncle, Mr. Charles F. Engleman, who was at that time quite a noted astronomer. This acquaintance rekindled a boyish love for mathematics and astronomy, and brought Ibach into special favor with this scientist. At the latter's death, in 1860, he left his unfinished publications to Ibach to finish, who, falling heir to all necessary books and charts, returned to Newmanstown to become an astronomer. From this place, for almost 30 years, he sent out his astronomical calculations and almanacs to many firms in our country and to a number in Cuba, South America, and other foreign countries. He furnished his publications in four different languages, French, English, Spanish and German.

A simple, unpretending frame house in this village constituted his home. In the rear of this was the philosopher's workshop, where were found all the appurtenances of such a scientist. Maps and charts upon the walls, mounted globes, telescopes, stacks of books, many of them rare and important, recounting astronomical observations of thousands of years ago, and giving reminiscences of the Ptolemies, Thales and Meton, or the opinions of Kepler, La Caille, Lambert, Huygens, Galileo and others, stocked well this study. From this room, and the master brain that ruled here, this humble village has for three decades had the distinction of catching a strange light from the sun, the moon, the planets and all the stars, and reflecting the same to all the quarters of our globe.

> "Full many a gem of purest ray serene,
> The dark unfathomed caves of ocean bear."

CHAPTER IX.

AN OLD INDIAN TRAIL.

HAVING in my last left my company in the heart of the antiquated hamlet of Newmanstown, reflecting upon the philosophic genius who here, "far from the madding crowd's ignoble strife," for so many years kept the noiseless, though not fameless, tenor of his way, I will start the march to-day on an old Indian trail that led right through this territory. As we are in search of ancient landmarks, we shall not pass by one that nature herself has built and in point of age and durability shall outlive the grandest monument reared by the hand of man. I want to point out the ineffaceable relic of barbaric America, when the elements, the wild beasts and the red men held exclusive sway over this valley. Indeed, this landmark is older than man or beast. It points to primitive time. It is the gap in the South Mountain, just south of the village last visited, through which pass, or "Kluft" (as the villagers prefer to call it), led the old trail of the savages from their village or settlement on the forks of the Susquehanna, where Sunbury is now located, to the Penn treaty grounds on the banks of the Delaware.

When the first settlers came to this valley from Scho-

harie County, N. Y., in 1723, there were Indian villages
or traces of them all through this valley. But the most
significant local settlement or centre of the aborigines
then was beyond the Kittatinny at Shamokin, now Sunbury, from whence led this trail in an almost direct line
to the settlement of the peaceful Quaker and h's friendly

THE "KLUFT" NEAR NEWMANSTOWN.

neighbors, these red-skinned brethren. This trail led
through the Kittatinny or Blue Mountain range, at the
Swatara gap, and from thence in a direct line to the
South Mountain pass or gap.

Along this route, almost identical with the pipe-line
which the Standard Oil Trust has since drawn trans-

versely across our valley, carrying another kind of fire and in liquid form—that representing the civilization of our day—the journeys on foot or on the backs of Indian ponies, were taken to and fro by these first monarchs of our then measureless forests. What an army of unlettered barbarians passed up and down this grand old mountain pass! What generations of unprogressive freemen here preceded us! What restless hordes prowled about this old landmark of nature when the day of civilization dawned upon this western hemisphere, as so many owls and bats flutter to their holes, or so many prowling panthers to their cavernous lairs at the approach of day! Over it they travelled with reluctant and oft defying feet, in search of other hunting grounds. Let us climb this pass together in recollection of all these events.

We need not be apprehensive of any danger, although the way seem weird and the inhabitants but few. We will be in no peril. The war-whoop of the last fighting savage has long since died away with a succession of echoes that have reverberated among the rocky mountain sides that hem us in. It may be that an occasional wild-cat and some stray fox may sometimes venture out of their hiding place to look for prey or to see what use their once exclusive domain is put to, yet these will not do any harm to innocent students of history. So let us proceed on our tramp unmolested.

From Newmanstown we go directly south, along one mile of the best piece of road of which this county can boast. It is as straight as a stretched line, having good post fences on either side, and wide as a Chicago boulevard. It is well-graded and kept in first-class repair. We think much credit must be due the Messrs. Long, who own most of the property along this rural avenue, and have lived for many years in wealth and luxury at the base of the mountain. Not long ago the senior brother died in his palatial home located here.

Besides being a farmer and stock-raiser, he was a wholesale commission merchant, with stores in New York City, where he usually spent his winters. Large ice houses are located here, in which are stored during the summer immense quantities of eggs and butter for winter sale. This business has made this man a millionaire, which large fortune has been partly spent in valuable local improvements of the character described.

Having reached the foot of the mountain, we here find a little peasant hut standing guard on the entrance of this Alpine-like pass. In front of it is a watering trough, into which a boisterous brooklet dashingly pours its crystal beverage. All along the up-grade of our winding roadway, we hear the babblings of a turbulent mountain brooklet, sending its waters in haste over its rocky bed, until it foams and murmurs like a panting thing of life driven by some deadly foe. Now it leaps in broken sprays over a steep precipice, then it dashes against some rocky barrier that completely turns its course. But on and on it flows, taking no time to rest on its way or to parley with its occasional visitors, only in the language of Tennyson's famous brook, keeping up its song:

"Men may come and men may go
But I flow on forever."

On either side of our rustic up-way are found small springs to feed this streamlet. The largest and most famous of these is what is called the "Gold Spring," which is about half way up the gap on the right-hand side of the road. It is worth a trip from any part of the country to dip one's cup into its placid depths and quaff the sparkling ice-cold draught, that has just bubbled up, through golden sands, from its subterranean fountain, whence all springs flow. Doubtless the Indian and the deer often slaked their thirst at this spring. At present it supplies the dam from which Newmanstown draws its water. Oh! for such a waterhead for Lebanon and some one to lead it into our homes!

As we ascend let us take notice of the formation of the hills about us. On the right hand a gigantic promontory frowns down upon us. For hundreds of feet the crest rises almost perpendicularly from this gap, and early in the afternoon casts its shadow into the cleft below. One of the prettiest sights in nature is to see this hill outline itself on an afternoon in charming elongations of its shadow upon the opposite hillside. It may be seen any sunny afternoon and for miles away.

The left-hand side of the hill has exhibitions of violent convulsions of nature in the formative period of the earth. Monstrous forces must have had free play here, judging from the way the mountains of bowlders are piled together. Rocks, many of them larger than

houses, are here rolled up on ledges that form the steps
of a giant's staircase up to its brow. To this summit
we may climb to find a little platform of huge rocks
higher than any other point, and known as Eagle's
Peak, where will be afforded us one of the most ex-
quisite views of this valley. Hundreds of people visit
this spot every summer and here take observations of
one of the most extensive and transporting realms of
rural and scenic beauty and agricultural wealth visible
in our state. He who climbs these heights some pleasant morning will always know what a vision Moses
must have had from Mt. Nebo's heights when he took
his first and only gaze into the Promised Land. Our
illustration shows a view too distant to do justice to
its nearer grandeur.

And this peak is itself an historic landmark. Hither
climbed, on March 22, 1751, "to view the landscape
o'er," the venerable patriarch of the American Lutheran Church, Rev. Dr. Henry Melchoir Muhlenberg, in
company with Rev. P. Brunnholtz, honored pastor of the
Lutheran congregations at Philadelphia and Germantown; Rev. J. C. Hartwig, on and out of whose large
real estate in Otsego Co., N. Y., was later established
the first Lutheran Theological Seminary in this country; Conrad Weiser, whose guests these were, and
others. The occasion was the pastoral conference, called
by Muhlenberg, and held at Weiser's house, to consider
the pastoral call which Muhlenberg had shortly before
received from the Dutch Lutheran congregation of New

York City, and to investigate the trouble between Pastor Handschuh and his flock at Lancaster. These men met at Reading a few days before, and proceeded together to Weiser's home at Tulpehocken. Dr. Mann in his "Life and Times of Muhlenberg," based upon such authoritative data as the patriarch's own diary, alludes to this event, on page 264 of his book, as follows:

"The following day the travellers arrived at Tulpehocken, and on March 22d, for bodily exercise, they, with some of the friends, ascended the highest point of the South Mountain, three miles distant from Weiser's residence, where a splendid panorama for a distance of thirty miles extended before them, limited to the west and the southwest by the Blue Mountain chain. The sun was shining, the sky was clear. Large rocks formed a protection against the March winds. Three eagles, probably having their nests in the lonely neighborhood, wheeled in circles above the heads of the strange visitors, rising higher and higher in the air until in the golden hues of the sunbeams they finally disappeared. This beautiful picture brought strange feelings to the hearts of the brethren, for it recalled to them the symbolic picture of the eagle couching in front of the wide-spreading golden rays of the sun on the Orphan-House at Halle. Many a Bible quotation having more or less bearing upon the occasion and the surroundings was then given, and some old German church-hymns were intoned on this lofty height, and carried the praises of God to His throne. They all felt it was good to be there. Unwillingly they left their grand elevation to climb down again into the valley over rock and precipice, and to resume the cares and troubles of a world of labor." What a grand spot this to hold, some summer day, the biggest reunion of Lutherans ever held in this country! Who knows but the Luther Leagues of Pennsylvania and New York, the two states then rivaling each other for Muhlenberg's services, may some day effect this!

Having now reached the top of our mountain road, through its environment of rocky, glen-cut mountain slopes, we reach a large table-land, or plateau, on the very top of the South Mountain. It extends for several miles in each direction. On this elevation is found the celebrated Texter farm, where its late proprietor and owner died recently, and concerning whose will and bequests there is now pending in the Lebanon County courts a somewhat interesting litigation suit. This farm at one time contained 1,900 acres, and though somewhat reduced, is still an immense plantation. On these heights, until recently, the last owner, Mr. Joel Texter, rivaled Mr. S. S. Long, at the base of the hill, in the raising of fine blooded stock. Each gained an extensive reputation and considerable wealth. But now both have departed to "the undiscovered country from whose bourn no traveler returns." With a better use made of their time and possessions, we trust, than their former savage owners, whose ancient highway led through both their tracts, they have gone to answer the summons of that Great Spirit, who gives to all of us, for a little while, power and opportunity.

CHAPTER X.

A CRADLE OF RELIGIOUS SECTS.

COMING down the "Delectable Mountains," from which we took our last enchanting view of the valley, by the same "Kluft" roadway we took in ascent, we will to-day wind our way westward along the meanderings of the Mill Creek—the stream that waters this section of the country and gives a name to the township. We will have a stretch of about five miles to go till we come to the fountain-head of this stream and the border line of Heidelberg township, the next adjoining. This little vale is a poem for natural beauty and improved cultivation. It deserves to be immortalized in song and history. To the writer's eye it has the appearance of a huge cradle, fashioned thus by nature and employed by providence in which to rock the infant life (on this continent) of no less than half a dozen of our Protestant religious denominations.

Let us first take our walk through this lovely vale, and then give the history of the foundings of these sects. The valley stretches in a westerly or southwesterly course from Newmanstown in the direction towards Schaefferstown. On our left, the towering South Mountain hems us in, which being so close at

7 (89)

hand clearly shows its every rocky rib, in the afternoon
sun, like some ill-fed, petrified mastodon. It also gives
a sense of warmth and protection to the dwellers that
cosily nestle in the rich vale at its feet, which helps the
imagination in seeing the cradle-likeness of this territory. On our west, a small ridge rises that, though
broken more or less, continues on to Schaefferstown,
and is parallel with the southern border hills. By a
slight pressure upon either barrier, methinks, and a little
stretch of the imagination, one can see this cradle rock.
It is covered during most of the year with one of Dame
Nature's homespun spreads of emerald hue, and reminds
one of the famous Tyrol valleys. Here many first settlers of the Lebanon valley planted their homes. They
came from different parts of Germany, and by different
routes, but arrived here about simultaneously, whether
by way of Schoharie, N. Y., or of Philadelphia, Germantown, and Conestoga. The rich quality of the land,
the abundance of water in springs and stream, and the
beauty of scenery, justify their sharpened wit in dis-
criminating choice.

Following the little mountain brooklet, that is born
of a hundred springs in the mountain sides of the Indian
Pass last described, until this empties into the Mill
Creek, we pass two old grist mills that serve as landmarks in this part of the vale in question. The first is
what is now generally known as the Cherrington Mill,
built in 1800, by Philip Kalbach, and for many years in
the proprietorship of the Cherringtons, Ezekiel, John

F., and James E., respectively, father, son, and grandson. The other mill is the Zimmerman mill, situated on the same mountain stream, but is not as old as the former. A short distance to the right is the Zeller fort, already described, where the German Lutherans had their beginning in American church life. Likewise the Reformed, a little beyond at Tulpehocken. On reaching the Mill Creek proper, we have but a mile to the hamlet known as Mill Creek Center, but by older citizens still spoken of as *Muehlbach*, the German for Mill Creek. Here also is located a mill, the oldest of all in the township, and this spot claims to have witnessed the very first settlement in these parts. Let us stop long enough in our ramble to visit the few points of interest.

First we will visit the church and graveyard. Here as early as 1747 the records show a joint Lutheran and Reformed church to have been erected. Before this time these settlers worshipped at Tulpehocken. This was the first church in all this Mill Creek Valley. It was a rude log meeting house, followed by a frame church, which in 1790 gave place to the present stone structure, situated on a slight elevation of ground. This latter building was remodeled a few years ago, during the centennial year of its erection, when by the expenditure of several thousand dollars it was changed into a beautiful modern church building in its exterior appearance and interior style and arrangements. A marble slab over the entrance door gives the above-named facts epito-

mized. Until recently a very old German Bible was
here used in services. The church has generally been
served by the Tulpehocken pastors on the Lutheran
side, and by the Schaefferstown pastors on the Reformed side. The graveyard surrounding the church
shows in its tombstone records the names of the surrounding citizens and the story of their constant gathering into this silent "city of the dead." One of the
oldest graves it contains that is marked by a legible
stone is that of Anderes Saltzgeber, of which the following is a fac-simile :

HIER RUHET
ANDERES SALTZ-
GEBER IST GEBOHREN
DEN 26 DEC 1708
GESTORBEN 1769
SEINES ALTERS 61
IAHR SEINE EHFR-
AV WAR ANN MA-
RIA EINE GEBOH-
RNE ZELERN. IN DE-
R EH GRLEBT 41 IAHR

But while this is the only church in this hamlet, it was not the first religious worship which its erection witnessed here. It is claimed that fully two decades or more before this time, Conrad Beissel and a few associate German Baptists, or Dunkards, arrived from Germany and settled here, doubtless conducting worship in the house this leader is said to have erected. It is evident that they here found water enough to accommodate them in their immersion practices. As no history of the erection of a Dunkard meeting-house or of a separate local congregation is extant, it is probable that this nucleus formed a part of the Conestoga First Day Dunkards. It was not long, however, before Mr. Beissel "fell out" with his brethren on a number of points of doctrine, principally that concerning the Sabbath observation, he claiming the Seventh day as the proper one to be kept. He published a tract as early as 1725, fully setting forth his views, and withdrew from fellowship with his brethren. He had quite a following, and thus was born the Seventh Day Baptist Sect or Society, which, led by their zealous leader, removed to Ephrata, Lancaster county, where they promulgated their mystic views, erected a convent, and made for themselves a quaint but somewhat conspicuous history among the denominations of our land. In education and publication this new center was leading the German population of this section of the state for a quarter of a century.

This hamlet contains another interesting landmark that we must visit ere we pass on. It is the old mill,

whose grist has fed man and fattened beast for almost a
century and a quarter.

A carved stone in the face of the wall, evidently provided with a receptacle for deposits of a documentary
character, like the corner-stones of churches, gives date
and name of builder as follows :

The house is a very fine and substantially built structure with wall of native red-sandstone and limestone,
dressed and trimmed, with broken or hipped Dutch roof,
and finished in massive style and in hard wood. The
stairway and hand-rail are of solid oak and still a thing
of beauty. The quaint and massive Queen Anne man-
telpiece is likewise of solid oak, as pretty as any quartered oak now in use. The doors and patent locks of
long ago still add charm to a landmark which is as well
kept and as cheerful a home as that of Mt. Vernon on
the banks of the Potomac. It is now the property of
Mr. E. R. Illig, whose family have occupied it for a
number of years. Tradition connects the romance of
an illicit love affair and escapade with the builder and
first proprietor. Rumor says that he fell in love with

his servant girl, and after some remonstrances against
this intimacy by his wife—the Maria Catharine of the
above engraved stone—Mr. Müler eloped with his para-
mour to Virginia, leaving the property to his upbraid-
ing wife and her family.

THE ILLIG HOME AND MILL IN MILL CREEK CENTRE.

It was presumably a son of this first couple, and his
wife, who erected in 1784 the mill property that is attached to this old stone mansion.　It is also of stone, in
the same style of architecture as the house, and has a
date-stone in the face of the wall exposed to the road-
side, which reads as follows:

```
17                      84

        GOTT ALEIN DEEN.
        ──────────
        MICHAEL MILLER
        MELISABET MILLER
```

There is some poetry and piety in the thought that a mill should serve God alone. Dedicated thus to God, it has served Him and man, we suppose, for a century and a decade of time. As far as we know, it has always ground its grist in peace and blessing, and we trust it may never grind out the wrath of Jehovah, or be made to prove that

"The mills of the gods grind slowly,
But they grind exceeding fine."

It was on the large farm in connection with this ancient mill property, that the enterprising and intelligent Illig family was reared, two of whom are the celebrated proprietors of a large dry goods store in Reading, while the farm has been divided among three others, whose lovely homesteads front on this Mill Creek road just outside of the village. The one is that of Mr. E. R. Illig, already described; next comes the house and farm of Capt. Batdorf, whose wife was an Illig; and the third, the original homestead, is that of Mr. Hiram L. Illig, who is renowned as being, without doubt, the possessor of the largest collection of Indian relics, (spearheads, lance-heads, scalping knives, scrapers, mortars, pestles and rude utensils and ornaments) in the county.

The arrangement of these relics is orderly and systematic according to the various strata of rock formation from which they were constructed. Concerning this branch of archæology their possessor is a master, and altogether this family is far above the average in rural intelligence. They would be leaders in, and a credit to any community.

A SECTION OF HIRAM L. ILLIG'S INDIAN RELICS.

But we must close this chapter and defer to the next one an account of the founding and earliest beginnings of the Evangelical Association, which took place in this valley, and the interesting landmarks concerning which are still found here.

CHAPTER XI.

I AM now ready to lead my readers to a two-fold fountain-head, the spot being the source both of the somewhat historic Mill Creek, along which we have been rambling in our last jaunt, and also of the Evangelical Association, which as a religious denomination has almost completed its first century of rather remarkable and checkered life. The same spring that gives birth to the above-named stream marks the spot also that brought into organic being this branch of the Protestant Church; for over this spring was built a house in which the organization was effected. It is a remarkable coincidence that another spring, feeding this same creek, farther down its current, marks the place where Elder Peter Becker, of the Dunkard persuasion, immersed Conrad Beissel, the rather illustrious founder of the Seventh Day Baptist sect, which spring is known in the denominational history of this church as the "Dunkard Spring;" while still further down this same stream is the Zeller house or fort, also built over a spring and emptying into the Mill Creek, where the German Lutherans of this country had their organic beginning.

Having left my readers at Mr. H. L. Illig's Bazar of

Aboriginal Archæology, or Indian Relics, we are but two miles from the fountain head we want now to visit. But these are two miles fraught with intensely interesting history. And although the current of history, like that of water, should be followed from its source downward and onward, it suits us best to go up

THE BECKER HOMESTEAD, MILL CREEK.

the streams of both, because along this way lies the chosen course of our historical excursion. Hence we come first to the Becker house, where the first annual conference of the Evangelical Association was held in 1807. This house is still standing on the next estate to Illig's, on the right-hand side of the road going to

Kleiufeltersville, and is more than a mile northeast of the other Becker homestead, where, in 1803, Bishop Albright called his followers together for mutual conference about separation from former church affiliations and organization into a new sect, by the adoption of rules and regulations, which led to the present discipline of this church and its entire mode of denominational life and polity. We will pick up the scraps of historic interest that lie along the way to this historic spot. The Becker estate originally consisted of 1,500 acres of land, the property of a Miss or Mrs. Jane Fenn, of Chester County, who leased it to parties resident here, and whose relatives would visit it in summer and fish along the creek that flowed through the plantation. There are still legal papers in the hands of the Becker family, showing the transfer of the property to a Mr. Becker, when the Penns found it did not pay them. Then the plantation was cut into smaller farms, and the different farm houses were built thereon. The one alluded to as the house in which the first annual conference of Albright's church was held, is a large, commodious, farm dwelling-house, built of regularly dressed sandstone of reddish tint that is quarried near by, and was erected, according to a date-stone in its wall, in 1770. Some alterations have been made since that first conference, but the large room, or rooms, in which the sessions of this historic gathering were held are intact and are still pointed out to the visitor. It was attended by five itinerant and three local preachers and twenty official lay members, and was continued for two days, November 15 and 16, 1807. At this meeting Albright was elected superintendent or first bishop of the society and instructed to formulate rules of discipline, which latter duty he was prevented from accomplishing by decline of health and an early, untimely death. In this house met also the third and fourth annual conferences of this association, and here were licensed a number of the first preachers of the body, who afterwards figured prominently in this church. The large yard and garden of this homestead has the noteworthy distinction of being so well fenced in that 127 years of frost and tempest have not shaken this original construction of shelter and protection. The posts are solid sandstone, of the same quality used in the walls of the house, are about one foot square, and stand four feet above ground. Into these are drilled holes, in which rest the rails. The one on which the gate swings has the following figure engraved on it, which is still quite legible:

The initials stand for George Becker, the builder.

Had the church here founded been as securely environed by a fence, strong enough to keep out pride and sin and foreign ideas, there would not be the sad litigations that now divide this once influential portion of Christ's body.

Leaving this place and still going on towards Kleinfeltersville, we pass the private burial place of several generations of this family, a Dunkard meeting-house, the fine home and farm of Rev. George Bucher, the Dunkard preacher of this district; and, crossing the line of Heidelberg township, we soon come to the fountain head of this creek, and the place where Albright's religious society was formed and where by a singular providence he died, May 18, 1808. This was the home of John George Becker, a son of the George Becker already alluded to, I think. The house in which he lived was also a sandstone dwelling, reared over the spring in question, and was originally provided with mere port-holes for windows, and used as a house of refuge from the Indians. It has recently been torn down and replaced by a double-story frame dwelling, where now lives Mr. Wm. Hoffman, who is married to a granddaughter of this friend of Albright's, a daughter of Rev. John Kleinfelter, who was married to John G. Becker's daughter.

Mr. Becker, being an early disciple of Albright's, opened his house for services and for the exercise of Christian hospitality towards these itinerants. Thus it came that in this house were witnessed on November 3, 1803, the birth of this society and the licensure of Rev. Albright, later the marriage of one of its daughters to Rev. Kleinfelter, one of these itinerant preachers and afterwards a presiding elder, and on May 18, 1808, the death of the first bishop, Rev. Albright.

Mr. Albright was a native of Montgomery, and during his ministry and at the time of his death was a resident of Lancaster County. He was returning from a quarterly conference held on Easter, 1808, in Albany, Berks county, suffering from a pulmonary affection, when, completely prostrated, he was compelled to stop on his way home at the house of Brother Becker, where he took his bed, and died a few weeks after. A few days after, May 20th, he was buried in the private burial plot of this Becker family, which plot was afterward erected into a church burial ground. His grave here is marked by a simple stone, of which the following is the epitaph:

Zum Gedächtnis
des
Ev. Pr. Jacob Albrecht
wurde geboren
den 1 ten May 1759
starb
den 18 ten May 1807
alt
49 Jahre u. 17 Tage.
Unter diesen Stein ruhen sein
Gebein.
Der Todt seiner Heiligen ist
Werth gehalten für dem Herrn.
Psalm 116, v. 15.

After Rev. Kleinfelter married Mr. Becker's daughter and came into possession of much of his property, he laid out the village of Kleinfeltersville, donated ground for an Evangelical church and graveyard, and was largely instrumental in having the East Pennsylvania Conference build a memorial church at this place in

ALBRIGHT MEMORIAL CHURCH.

honor of the energetic bishop, who died and lay buried here. Accordingly, in 1850, kept by the Evangelical Association as a year of jubilee, this church was erected. The conference appointed Revs. J. P. Leib, J. M. Saylor and F. Sanner to supervise the work. It is a very modest structure of red sandstone, of rather small dimensions, after the simple style adopted by this denomination in that day of extreme simplicity. It is surmounted by a small cupola, in which swings a little bell. On its front a marble slab tells the following story:

ALBRECHT'S KIRCHE
Errichtet
Zum Andenken des verewigten
JACOB ALBRECHT
Stifter der Evangelischen Gemeinschaft
in Nord America
Im 50ten Jahre der Gemeinschaft
ANNO 1850.
Ganz neu aufgebaut im Jahr 1860

Few people worship here at present and fewer still are the visits to the adjoining graveyard, though there would be for a Gray another Elegy here.

After devoting about twelve years to the itinerancy and the office of presiding elder, with a district stretching from Philadelphia to the Ohio River, Rev. Kleinfelter retired and carried on a mercantile business at this place and in the neighboring village of Flickinger, Lancaster county, the remainder of his life. He lies buried in the same rustic graveyard, not far from Albright's grave; and his wife, who as a child must have ministered to the dying bishop, sleeps by his side. Their tombstones are more pretentious, and the epitaphs read as follows:

8

REV. JOHN KLEINFELTER.
Born May 5, 1791.
Died April 16, 1863.
Aged 71 years 11 Mo. 11 da.

He became an active and influential
member of the Evangelical denomination at the early age of 20 years,
when that Church was yet struggling
in its Infancy, and by his Christian
life he became a Power, felt throughout the entire Brotherhood. Filling
the various positions of circuit Preacher, Elder, &c. Thus improving every
opportunity to do good, and become
good.

J. E. D.

OUR MOTHER
CATHARINE
WIFE OF
REV. JOHN R. KLEINFELTER
Daughter of
GEORGE AND MARIA BECKER.
Born April 1, 1796.
DIED
June 13, 1883.
AGED
87 Years 2 Mo. 12 Days.
Text 2 Timothy 4: 7-8.

H. L D.

Her father also lies buried here.   His grave stone is :

In memory of
JOHN GEORGE BECKER,
Born Sept. 29, 1767,
Died Nov. 16, 1855,
etc., etc.

And here at this humble graveyard, where sleep these early and pious workers of a denomination that has wielded an extensive influence in the first century of its existence, we must part company for a short time.

CHAPTER XII.

THE COUNTY'S OLDEST TOWN.

To-day I want to take my readers, whither a kind friend has recently taken me, to the oldest town within the limits of Lebanon county, if not of this valley. About the same time (perhaps a year or two before) the Schoharie Germans settled in this valley, the wave of German immigrants, which flowed by way of Philadelphia and the lower counties of Montgomery, Chester and Lancaster, began to break over the border hills that separate the Lebanon and East Penn valleys from the Lancaster valley, and poured down this barrier's northern slope into the narrow vales that lie betwixt the foot-hills of this South Mountain range. Thus as early as 1720 the log cabins of these first settlers began to rise in the wild forests of these foot-hills. Soon one wave of immigration followed another and before two decades had passed, quite a flood of German colonists had poured over the Suabian hills into our south-eastern county borders and spread itself out in the present south-ernmost townships of Mill Creek, Heidelberg, South Lebanon, Cornwall and Londonderry. Heidelberg, the settlement, assumed the first town-nucleus, and accordingly Heidelberg-town, or what for the past century has been known, by the name of its founder, as Schaefferstown, justly claims the distinction of being the first town "laid out" and built up within the county. It is located but two miles west or southwest from where I took leave of my readers in the last chapter.

Whatever clusters of houses and settlements may have been formed before, the town was regularly laid out by Alexander Schaeffer in 1744. He had first taken up his abode in the foot-hills already alluded to, where at a recent date his log cabin, built about 1738, was still standing. From thence he removed to the site of the present town, where he had bought a large tract of land, which he immediately proceeded to lay out into a town plot after the present plan of a central market square and four principal streets leading out thence.

Here he raised his family, the descendants of which are still found hereabouts. One great-grand-daughter is married to William Dissinger of town, and another, the daughter of Abraham Rex, long a successful local merchant, is the widowed wife of the late Wm. M. Weigley, Esq., whose magnificent brown-stone mansion graces the streets of this ancient *burg*, conspicuously towering over its lines of humble dwellings.

The body of Schaeffer lies buried in the portion of the cemetery where the Reformed buried their dead, and about him are buried his family. The hands of considerate descendants have since marked these graves with becoming tombstones. That of the founder himself contains the following epitaph :

Hier ruht
Im Herrn der Leib des
ALEXANDER SCHEFFER
Ift gebohren den 8ten
Janvarivs 1712
Ift geftorben den 10ten
April 1786
Alt worden 74 Iahr
5 Monath & Zwey tage
Amen.

Schaefferstown is a rich field for the antiquarian. It is built on more hills than the Eternal City, and, but for the lack of that city's charming Tiber, might have rivaled Rome itself. In scenic beauty of mountain and farm-land, and in the fascinating romance of its interesting history, it lacks nothing to rival any town of more pretentious boast.

Let me take my readers to the crest of the highest hill and point out objects of historic interest. As we desire in these trips to dwell among the ancient and the past, it is fitting that we take this position, for here is located the resting place of these worthy departed ones, hundreds upon hundreds of whom have been gathered on this northern hill-side to sleep side by side, like so many children, who, wearied of play, have fallen asleep in a mother's arms, and by her been gently tucked into their little beds for the night.

What a melancholy spot is an ancient graveyard! What food for sober and solemn meditation here! If it afford at the same time, as does this one, an outlook over the farms and work-shops, where the sleepers beneath the sod once toiled, what an observatory for the spirit of man to take bearings of life—its past, present, and future! One need not read the solemn exhortations engraved upon the tombstones to feel serious; all the atmosphere is solemnly hortatory, and a host of earnest spirits arise to admonish a reflecting mind to think of life soberly and to live it wisely and well.

Before we walk among the dead, however, and read their epitomized biographies, preserved in engraven epitaphs, let us look out upon the scenes of activity, where this brave and gallant peasantry—fugitives from tyranny, persecution and bigotry—laid the foundations of this valley's present day prosperity. To the east stretches the beautiful valley of the Mühlbach with its rich farms—to the south the rolling hills covered with tilled fields break like waves of the sea against the South Mountain ridge. To the west, bordered on the south by the Cornwall hills, roll the farms, one against the other, till they are lost in the hazy distance; and from the northwest, in the direction of Lebanon, to the northeast, in the direction of Richland, there is afforded an extensive sweep of the very paradise of agricultural richness and beauty. At our feet lies the ancient village, where are still preserved a very large proportion of the primitive habitations in which dwelt the humble-minded forefathers that now sleep beneath our feet. Altogether the scenery is intensely beautiful, sufficiently wild and varied to give it a charm not possessed by a tame, monotonous stretch of landscape, yet sufficiently tamed and enriched by the hands of thrifty German husbandmen—the peaceful monarchs of our valley—to make most of it as pretty as a finished picture, or as lovely as a garden.

From the south leads the Lancaster road, passing through such old towns as Lititz and Brickerville and by the celebrated Elizabeth furnaces, about three miles away, which were erected about 1755 by one John Huber, but later purchased by Baron Henry W. von Stiegel, of Manheim, Pa., a wealthy native of Manheim, Germany, who here made shot and shell, and cast guns for the Provincial army during Revolutionary times. Stiegel conducted this industrial plant for about eighteen years, manufacturing the old-fashioned jamb stoves, said to have borne the following legendary inscription:

"Baron Stiegel ist der Mann
Der die Ofen giesen Kann."

While engaged in this business he built a residence and tower in Schaefferstown, and laid out the southern portion, now known as "Canada." The first hill one-fourth of a mile south of the town center marks the spot where this castle tower or *Thurm* stood, and from it received the name of *Thurm-berg* or "Tower-hill."

The tower has gone into decay, but old citizens remember it, and relate that in it the Baron himself taught school in later days, when his fortune had taken wings. One of his sons removed to the Shenandoah Valley, Virginia, and there married, had issue and became wealthy. There are still descendants living in those parts who have in recent years visited these scenes made famous by their illustrious sire. It is doubtless through this southern connection that many of the blooded Virginia and Maryland horses came to be tried in the once celebrated race-tracks located about two miles south of the town, giving this settlement notoriety a century before this sport did the same for New Jersey politicians.

The "Tower-hill" marks also two other spots of historic interest. The one is the Jewish cemetery on its southern slope, where were buried the first colonists of this community, who were Jews, and who were at one time strong enough to have a synagogue and maintain worship. While the spot of the "Jewish church" and graveyard can still be identified, it is a shame that there should here be found such inconsiderate vandalism as to lay its unholy hands upon the walled enclosure of this sacred spot, and reduce to the common level of a field or orchard what should have been kept as holy ground and been most jealously guarded as an historic relic. The other spot of interest on Tower-hill is the spring which has for nearly 150 years supplied this town with water. It is located on the northern slope of this hill

just on the edge of town, is walled over into a reservoir
and shaded by giant oaks and maples, through whose
out-spreading branches the spring winds still whistle
songs of "the forest primeval." An artificial park
is slowly forming about the same, with seats and band-
stand to entice, on summer nights, the villagers to
its cooling retreat. This best of water supplies has

A SCHAEFFERSTOWN WATERING TROUGH.

been utilized since 1753 as a public water works, so
deeded by the founder of the town and his wife to appointed trustees for the use of inhabitants of Market
Square and street. It claims to be the first public water
works established in the United States. Two public
fountains have poured their clear, sparkling and never-

failing contents into immense watering troughs for 141 years to gladden man and beast.

Down by this Lancaster roadway, past the furnace, race track, Jewish cemetery, baronial castle and "leading spring" of Schaeffer's, the Lancaster and Womelsdorf postman, for many a year before the close of the last century, drove into town with his tally-ho and freight of passengers, parcels and post, announcing his arrival into town by the sounding of his bugle-horn. We will let an imaginary blast of this trumpet interrupt our observations and call us from our heights into the town below, where we shall gather additional facts of history. But for this we must wait, inasmuch as the limit of this chapter has already been reached.

CHAPTER XIII.

AMONG OLD GRAVES AND BUILDINGS.

THE bugle-blast of the old-time postman interrupted our historic search in the last chapter. It summoned us while on the sacred hillside of Schaefferstown, where the community has buried half a dozen generations of sturdy peasantry and noble yeomaury together. Before we take leave of this spot let us take a look at the stones that mark their sepulture. What a field of moldering bones and bleaching marble is this "God's acre!" The stately shaft of granite or marble is found side by side with the low and crumbling limestone marker or the lichen-covered sandstone, as the bones of those interred underneath commingle into a common dust. Here are found the graves of nearly all who have lived in this vicinity for a sesqui-centennium. Here, indeed, meet together the rich and poor of the Lord, who is the Maker of them all!

After passing the graves of the Moyers and Rexes, and the fine Weigley monument of granite, surmounted by a womanly figure in marble showering flowers from her hand, we come into the older portion of the burial ground, where the Schaeffers and Wolfersbergers and Erpffs are buried. We take especial interest in the tombs of the last-named family, consisting of parents and one daughter, deceased in childhood, because of the elaborate tombstone erected over this child's grave, and because of the story of the life and good will of the parents. According to the account of an aged informant, Mrs. Jere. Steinmetz (*nee* Mock), whose uncle was a beneficiary of this benevolent pair, Mr. and Mrs. Philip Erpff (Erb?) emigrated to this country as redemptioners, and served their years of bondage ("bound out") along the Mühlbach. By·industry and perseverance they gained a competency and became the possessors of a profitable farm near town. After the death of their only child they made a will, bequeathing, after death, the sum of fifty pounds sterling to all of their god-children, and the residue of their estate to the Lutheran church of the town, of which they were members. It is said, however, that after the wife's death, which occurred first, outsiders interfered with the husband, and, either by an alteration in the will ·or crookedness in the estate's settlement, the church was deprived of this intended legacy. It is a pity that to prevent this specious form of embezzlement, all benevolently disposed men and women have not yet learned how to become their own executors! The following are facsimiles of the tombstones of Mr. Erpff and his daughter, the wife's being similar to his. We ask the readers to notice the artistic elaboration expended upon this pet child's memorial stone, and consider the age in which it was erected:

```
             Hier
      Ruhen die gebeine von
    PHILIP JACOB  ERPFF
    Gebohren zu Geyfzeugen
         im Hertzogthum
    Wurtemberg den 20ten
        October A. D. 1724
      Gestorben den 30ten
      Iauuarius A. D. 1803
      Sein Alter 78 Iahr
    3 Monaten und 10 tage
```

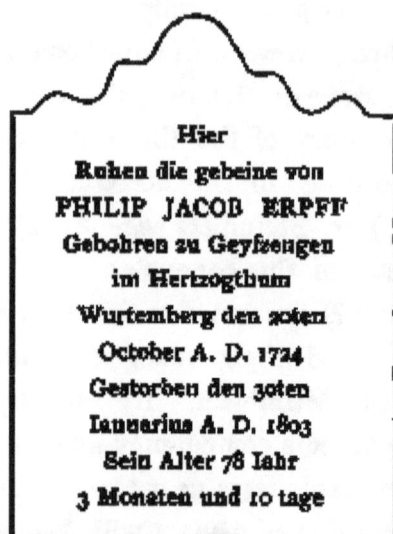

The child's grave is marked by a sandstone fully seven inches thick and about three and a half feet high. The sculptor of that day must have here done his best to please the living and properly honor the dead. Here is a sample of his art. It seems to represent life and death, as the head of the tomb-stone is to represent a living face, and at the bottom of it death is pictured in the skull and cross-bones. We desire also to call the attention of the reader at the ancient sign of the duplication of a letter as found in the words "Erpf," "Susana" and "Auo." Many similar specimens of this common usage of duplication abound in the old grave-yards visited. But the roof-like shape of the top of stone is something rare. It is seldom found. We present in the following cut a fair representation of this elaborate and unique ancient memorial stone :

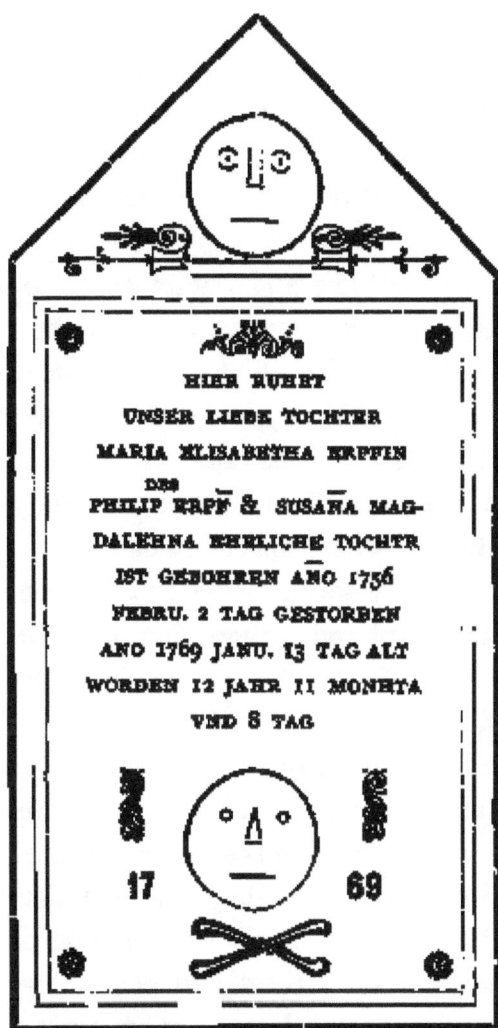

HIER RUHET
UNSER LIEBE TOCHTER
MARIA ELISABETHA ERPFIN
DES
PHILIP ERPF & SUSANA MAG-
DALEHNA EHELICHE TOCHTR
IST GEBOHREN ANO 1756
FEBRU. 2 TAG GESTORBEN
ANO 1769 JANU. 13 TAG ALT
WORDEN 12 JAHR 11 MONETA
VND 8 TAG

17   69

Now passing the graves of Peter Sheetz and Philip Wolfersberger, who with others in this community used to be the owners of negro slaves before their freedom was legally granted in our state, let us descend into the ancient town lying at our feet.

With the exception of a few additions in the form of handsome and costly homes, in modern styles of architecture, such as the Weigley mansion, the residence of Dr. Zerbe and others, and a new Reformed church edifice and a remodeled Lutheran church building, we will find the town very much as it was fifty years ago. The language, customs and habits of the people have not changed. To one who comes from the current of our busy, whirring life of steam and electricity and steam-harnessed machinery, everything here seems new and strange because it is so tame and antiquated. But this does not necessarily make against the place. It only furnishes us with a specimen of life in the generations when honesty was a virtue and common brotherhood an established and realized fact, and a man's word as good as a bond or seal. Hence about the best way for our Pennsylvania German folk to go back in history a few generations and pay a visit to their honest and industrious forefathers, and look in upon their quiet and peaceful mode of life, is to spend a while in the Schaefferstown of to-day. Here they will find a simplicity of living undisturbed by such modern concomitants of civilization as labor strikes and commonweal armies and all that ferment of discontent among the laboring classes now sending its scummy ebullitions to the surface elsewhere. The master and the servant have here not yet exchanged places. The capitalist carries on whatever humble industry he has planned and set on foot, without fear of having a band of jealous ruffians and insolent vagrants shut up its doors. Wagons are built here as strong and reliable as when they were used to carry the surplus grain from the surrounding acres to Philadelphia.

The shoemaker has not yet learned to make his product out of shavings, but still makes shoes out of leather intended to be worn and not to increase the sale. And the school teacher—blessed paradise for this much-abused and law-circumscribed benefactor—can here wield his birch, if occasion demand it, without that mark of his patrons' appreciation which gives the pedagogue elsewhere an unsolicited course in law for giving his pupils an inevitable "course in sprouts." So lives Schaefferstown to-day, and so lived our fathers everywhere many years ago.

Coming down from our cemetery heights to see it, we take the street or lane that brings us to the Lutheran church and parochial school house of long ago—two of the oldest structures in the town. Both are built of limestone, and were erected in 1765, as is shown by an arched stone that was the head-stone of the main entrance to the church before its recent remodeling, where it was left to tell its story of antiquity when these entrance doors beneath it were walled out. The schoolhouse has for many years past been used for Sunday-school and mid-week devotional purposes.

This church has quite a history. As early as 1720, there are evidences of official burial services having been conducted here by missionary pastors. Frag-

9

mentary records prove that Rev. F. A. C. Muhlenberg at one time (1770-73) exercised pastoral functions here. Doubtless a log or frame church edifice must have ex-

SCHAEFFERSTOWN LUTHERAN CHURCH.

isted before the present stone structure. While the present building was erected, the congregation formed a part of the Tulpehocken pastorate, and Rev. John

Nicholas Kurtz was pastor.   He was succeeded by Rev.
C. Emanuel Shultze, from 1770 to 1809, who was assisted by his brother-in-law from 1770 to 1773 as stated.
Shultze was succeeded by the Rev. Wm. Baetes, from
1810 to 1836; by Rev. Jonathan Ruthrauff, from 1837
to 1849; by Rev. J. M. Dietzler, from 1850 to 1865;
by Rev. U. Graves, from 1865 to 1866; by Rev. G. J.
Martz, from 1867 to 1878; and by Rev. M. Fernsler,
from 1879 to the present time.   The congregation has
been part of four or five separate pastoral charges.   In
1865 it celebrated the centennial of the church erection,
when addresses were delivered by such well-known divines as Drs. E. Huber, Daniel Schindler, Revs. J. M.
Dietzler, E. S. Henry, and U. Graves.   In 1884, the
church was completely remodeled at considerable expense, the old steeple taken down from its west end
and built up at the east end, while sixteen feet were
added to its length on the west.   While the same solid
masonry stands and constitutes the wall, the building
has lost its antique appearance, and has assumed a modern style of architecture within and without.   A very
old pipe organ is still in use here.   The old communion
service bears this inscription: "Michael Weber und
seine Ehefrau Anna Barbara haben die Communion
Kanthen, in die Evangelish-Lutherische Kirche in
Heidelberg, Linkester Amt gestisset, 1764."
    The bell which used to swing in the old steeple,
and whose silvery tone for many years called this community to worship, is said to have had the following in-

scription: "Pack and Chapman, of London, Fecit 1773. For the Lutheran church, Heidelbergtown, Lancaster county." Similar ones were made by the same firm and at the same time for the Trinity Lutheran church of Lancaster city, and Salem Lutheran church, Lebanon. They were doubtless ordered by Rev. F. A. C. Muhlenberg, who was then the pastor in charge.

Contemporaneously with the Lutheran church, the Reformed congregation of town grew up. Their first church was a frame structure. Another of stone superseded this in 1796, which has in turn been displaced, in 1858, by a beautiful and imposing brick edifice, fronting on the Main street.

We are indebted to Dr. Egle's history of Dauphin and Lebanon county for the specimen lottery ticket, giving us an idea of how the second edifice and that of the old Reformed church, Lebanon, were paid for; a common resort for revenue in public enterprises of that day:

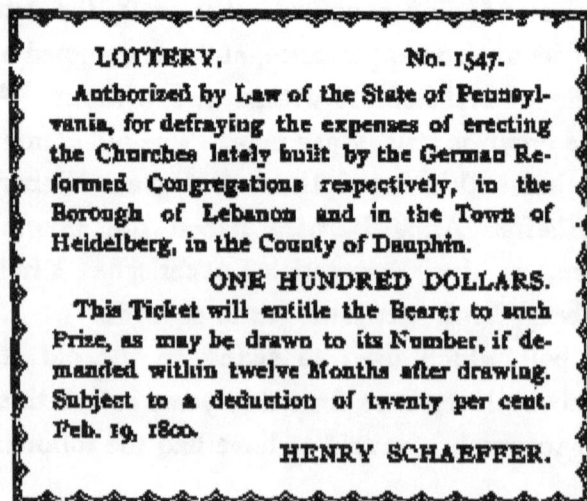

LOTTERY.   No. 1547.

Authorized by Law of the State of Pennsylvania, for defraying the expenses of erecting the Churches lately built by the German Reformed Congregations respectively, in the Borough of Lebanon and in the Town of Heidelberg, in the County of Dauphin.

ONE HUNDRED DOLLARS.

This Ticket will entitle the Bearer to such Prize, as may be drawn to its Number, if demanded within twelve Months after drawing. Subject to a deduction of twenty per cent. Feb. 19, 1800.

HENRY SCHAEFFER.

The known pastors of the Reformed church have been Revs. J. B. Rieger, Thomas Leinbach, Sr., Samuel S. and Thomas C. Leinbach, Jr., S. S. Sweitzer, J. A. Shultz, A. H. Leisse, and A. J. Bachman, the present incumbent.

In walking along these ancient streets one still sees a large number of the first peasant abodes, mere huts, whose low roofs can be touched with one's hand from the sidewalk. Most of these abodes are still occupied, but some are going into decay. Many are covered with tiles, and in view of these tokens of age, the town reminds one of Newmanstown.

The town center contains a spacious square or market place, along which are old buildings. One especially claims our attention. It is the old stone hostelry, erected in 1752 by the founder of the town. In ante-Revolutionary times it had a royal name, "King George," and sheltered many an aristocratic guest. After the Revolution, the sign portrait was changed from King George to that of George Washington. The most remarkable feature about this old landmark probably is its elaborately and well-built cellar. Its ceiling consists of a series of well-walled and cemented arches, receding from a common center. It is known to have on several occasions sheltered the inhabitants of the community from the depredations of the savages in the first and second decades after its erection.

Bidding adieu to this ancient town, we will take our way across the country towards Myerstown. Leading through the very paradise of Lebanon county farms, we will pass the palatial country residence and improved farms of Mr. Isaac Long, a brother and partner in the New York wholesale commission business of the late

KING GEORGE HOTEL, SCHAEFFERSTOWN.

S. S. Long, of Newmanstown. This summer residence is located at the corner where Mill Creek, Heidelberg and Jackson townships meet. A little nearer Myerstown we pass an ancient house, now occupied by Mr. Ezra Spangler, which has not gone out of the family hands since its erection. Though having signs of age upon it, it is in a good state of repair, and its fine lime-

stone walls are as substantial as when it was first built.
It bears in its front elevation a sandstone with the following quaint inscription, the quotation of which somber, semi-religious, orthographically-faulty sentiment
will close this chapter :

```
GOTT - GESEGNE - DIESES - HAVS - VND
WER - DA - GEYT - EIN - VND AVS - ICH GE
AVS - ODER - EIN - SO - STET - DER - DOTT
VND - WARTET - MEIN .'. 17 - 8a.
JACOB - SPENLER & E - S - B - S - F - R - N
```

CHAPTER XIV.

THE TULPEHOCKEN REFORMED CHURCH.

HAVING worked our way back to the Berks and Dauphin turnpike—fortunately for our jaunts, when such snows visit this region in the middle of April as the one that blocked up travel by steam, electricity, bicycle or foot last week—let us go down this ever passable highway to where we left it almost two months ago for our "round-about" excursion, and let us from this point work our way westward toward Lebanon, picking up along the way the scattered leaves of unwritten history. So we will go about three miles east of Myerstown to the oldest and one of the most important churches of the Reformed denomination in all this valley. It is known as the Tulpehocken Reformed church, and has a long and intensely interesting history. Because of its having been served by the two Leinbach brethren, Thomas H. and Charles, for over half a century, it is commonly spoken of as the "Leinbach Kirche."

It is located just west of the Tulpehocken Lutheran church, about a mile and a half west of Stouchsburg, along the turnpike, near a little village that has grown up recently under the name of Cocena. It is situated

ou rising ground, like that of the Lutheran church near
by, along a bend of the Tulpehocken creek, while the
two historic and venerable sites, with their sacred
temples and burial grounds and ancient parsonages,
frown at or greet one another (as the heart of the ob-

TULPEHOCKEN REFORMED CHURCH.

server is filled with bigotry or fraternity) from their
opposing hill-sides, like the ancient mountains of Ebal
and Gerizim.   We trust they have both been " mounts
of blessing " during all the hundred and fifty years of
gospel light that crown them.   It would seem at least

as if the earliest settlers that worshiped here desired that these sacred spots might prove Gerizims and not Ebals, where many of them built their houses even with a version of the promised Mosaic blessing (Deut. xxviii. 6) engraved upon them, "Gott gesegne dieses Haus, und wer da gehet ein und aus."

With no fear of having curses heaped upon us, let us repair to the spacious, stone manse that stands a little off the roadway, to the south. Although the present genial dominie, Rev. H. J. Welker, has a little farm of thirty acres to superintend, beside his parish work, we will find him none too busy to give us a little time and lead us into the very interesting past and present of all this sacred and historic landmark. The pastors here have been busy men from time immemorial, some of them having served as many as sixteen widely scattered congregations at one time, besides managing a mill property and the farm, which were then parts of the pastoral estate. The "church mill" has in recent years been disposed of and now turns its grist for another than the pastor. But a famous stone quarry on the premises still yields a handsome royalty as a revenue for the church.

The parsonage is a fine stone structure, commodious and kept in good repair. The wide hall-way and the cheerful rooms on either side bespeak welcome and comfort. They have done so to many thousand visitors during the more than a century of the manse's existence. Perhaps the most distinguished guest it ever sheltered was the late Dr. Philip Schaff, a native of Switzerland. His great learning early gave him a transcontinental reputation, and in 1844 he was called by the German Reformed church, of America, to fill a professorship in the institutions at Mercersburg, Pa. He landed in New York in July of that year, and taking up a leisurely journey towards the place of destination, he passed through Eastern Pennsylvania, stopping at Kutztown, Reading, and at Tulpehocken with Dr. Thomas H. Leinbach, the pastor. He probably spent a few days at this hospitable Reformed manse. He said of it a year before his death, at a meeting of the Reformed Synod in Reading, October, 1892, which he attended, that "the manners and customs of the people and the Pennsylvania-German dialect were exceedingly interesting" to him. This visit occurred the first day of August, 1844, nearly fifty years ago, and he arrived at Mercersburg August 12th, after stopping with Judge Bucher at Harrisburg, where, at a convention of Dutch and German Reformed delegates, he first met Dr. J. W. Nevin, with whom he was thenceforward to be so intimately connected as a colleague. It must be a source of just pride to every member of this flock that loves and knows how to appreciate the intellectually great, and especially for the pastor, to remember that this their pastoral abode once sheltered such a prince of theologians and church historians.

In the parsonage are found minute and extensive records of the labors of its pastors and the transactions

of this congregation. They cover three or four large
volumes, but the oldest and most valuable of all has
been lost. Still quite a full history of the church life
here can be constructed from the records at hand.
There have been three churches since the beginning
in 1744. The first one was a log building, and stood in
the southeast corner of the old cemetery. The second
church was built of stone, and stood opposite the road
from the present site, at the northwest corner of the orchard, between the pike and the parsonage. The
present edifice is a large two-story massive structure,
built of nicely dressed limestone. It bears in its front
elevation a marble slab containing the following engraving:

> REBUILT A. D. 1853.
> "THIS IS NONE OTHER THAN
> THE HOUSE OF GOD."
> THOMAS H. LEINBACH, MINISTER.
> BOARD OF TRUSTEES:
> Thomas Bassler, President.
> J. Steward, D. Moaser,
> Wm. Tice, J. Tice, H. Haack and M. Haack.
> BUILDING COMMITTEE:
> George Diehl, Jonathan Klopp
> and Eli Klopp.
> S. McAlister, Master Carpenter.

Although the building is not antiquated in its exterior
or interior arrangements, yet the congregation has

already decided to spend about $5,000 in its remodeling in the near future. (This was executed in 1894.) The following pastors have served this church : Prior to 1747, it was served for some little time by certain itinerant or missionary pastors, with an occasional sermon by Revs. Rieger, Boehm and George Michael Weiss, at intervals of six and twelve weeks. After 1747, the church had settled pastors, as follows:

Rev. D. Bartholmaeus, 1747-1750; Rev. H. W. Stoy, 1752-1755; Rev. Waldschmidt, 1757-1758; Rev. Otterbein, 1758-1764; Rev. John J. Zufall, 1765-1769; Rev. J. William Hendel, Sr., 1769-1782; Rev. Andrew Loretz,. 1785-1786; Rev. D. Wagner, 1787-1793; Rev. William Hendel, D. D., 1793-1823; Rev. Thomas H. Leinbach, 1826-1864; Rev. Charles H. .Leinbach, D. D., 1864-1883; Rev. Henry J. Welker, 1884 ——.

Of these pastors, as far as we could learn, but two are buried here, viz., the Leinbach brothers, a visit to whose graves we will mention in the next chapter. There are a few graves among the many hundreds of our German folk, who sleep in the two large and well-kept graveyards here, that claim our attention to-day. In the old cemetery, south of the pike, close by where the first church stood, are buried the Spychers, who were historical characters in the first half and middle of the last century. Benjamin, at whose house Col. Conrad Weiser gathered his regiment of 300 German farmers to repel the invading savages, already alluded to, was the illustrious ancestor of the Decherts and Neads of this valley

and that of the Cumberland. He was the son of John
Peter Spycher, and emigrated to America from the
Palatinate in 1738, settling in this neighborhood. In
1744 he was licensed as an Indian trader. He served as
an officer in the Provincial army during the French and
Indian war, and at the beginning of the Revolution
assisted in organizing the Berks county militia. He
was a member of the Provincial Conference of June 8,
1776, and of the Constitutional Convention of July 15,
1776. His grave is supposed to be among the Spycher
tombs found here, but the epitaph time has obliterated.

The grave of Peter Spycher, doubtless a brother of
Benjamin, is marked by a granite slab that is evidently
more recent than his death and, therefore, still quite
legible. He was among the men who figured prominently in arousing the Provincial Government to make
efforts of defense against the depredations of the Indians
in his day. A letter is still extant which he wrote
November 16, 1755, to Col. Conrad Weiser, then in
Philadelphia on public business, in which he describes
the recent depredations and butcheries among their
brethren by the Indians, including the slaughter of the
watch and many others, at Diedrich Six's (back of Millersburg). The letter closes as follows:

"I have this account from those above named, and from Peter An-
spach, John Caderman, Christopher Noacre, Leonard Walborn, George
Dollinger and Adam Dieffenbach.

"We are, at present, in imminent danger to lose our lives or estates.
Pray, therefore, for help, or else whole Tulpehocken will be laid
waste, by the Indians, in a very short time,—all the buildings will be

burned, the people scalped. Do, therefore, lose no time to get us assistance. The Assembly may learn from *this work*, what kind and fine *friends* the Indians are! We hope members of the Assembly will get their eyes opened and manifest tender hearts towards us ; and the Governor the same. They are, it is hoped, true subjects to our King George II, of Great Britain, or are they willing to deliver us into the hands of these cruel and merciless creatures?

"I am your friend,   PETER SPYCHER."

From a German paper, printed by C. Sauer, of Germantown, July, 1757, this Peter Spycher is mentioned as one of the three persons to whom any free-will contributions might be sent to aid in the better defense of the Tulpehocken and Bethel inhabitants against the savages, for which this paper then sent out a strong appeal to the German brethren, scattered all over the older portion of the province.

This Peter Spycher lived near Stouchsburg, and is buried in this old Reformed burial ground. His tombstone has the following inscription :

Zum Gedachtnifs
von PETER SPUCKER
Esq!
Gebohren Den 27 October
1711. Gestorben Den 13
Juli 1789
Ift alt worden 77 Jahr 8 Mo.
v ein halben

Among the oldest legible tombstone inscriptions we found the following, showing that the dead were buried here already in 1745:

HIR BEGRABEN
IOHANNES KIDZ
MILLER IST OF
BOHREN 1692
DEN 2 FEBRV
AR 11 GEST
ORBEN 1745

Here are also buried the founders of Myerstown and other leaders of long ago, of whom we will speak later.

CHAPTER XV.

AN HOUR WITH REFORMED PASTORS.

HAVING taken a general survey of the grounds and buildings and the past history of the Tulpehocken Reformed church, let us take our seat on the front portico of the historic parsonage, and in company with the hospitable dominie in charge, call up the long line of the sainted pastors who labored here in the past century and a half, and look them one by one into the face. The spring sun is genial, the zephyrs breathe gently through the boughs of the apple orchard, fast budding into leaf and blossom about us, and the crocuses and daffodils are near by to illustrate our faith in the first resurrection of the pious dead, while robins and song-sparrows help to lure us into an hour of memorial reverie and review. By the aid of some magic wand let us then call up the slumbering prophets, and while they may look in upon our latter life of modern improvements, we will catch, we trust, a sense of their piety and self-denial, while we gaze for an hour into their once familiar countenances.

The first that must be called up are those earliest supply-pastors, or missionaries, who preached the Gospel here before the first synodical organization of this denomination was effected in this country. These were

10 (137)

the Revs. Rieger, Boehm and Weiss, names that stand
high in the earliest annals of the Reformed church in
America. They were the very earliest pastors of this
church, and did much pioneer work for this denomination in Pennsylvania. Boehm began to preach in 1726,
before he was formally licensed. He took up his home

THE TULPEHOCKEN REFORMED PARSONAGE.

in Whitpain township, then Philadelphia county, about
sixteen miles north of that city, from whence he supplied surrounding places, even Philadelphia. At this
place (Whitpain) he built up a flourishing church that
still bears his name. Weiss located at Skippach, Mont-

gomery county, after arriving in this country with fifty
families of native Palatines, September 21, 1727, having been sent hither as the first ordained pastor of the
Reformed church in Pennsylvania, by "the upper con-
sistory, or classis, of the Palatinate." He served all the
older congregations of the upper end of Montgomery
county, such as Old and New Goschenhoppen, Gross–
Schwam, etc. He also visited the Fatherland, with one
Reif, in the interests of the struggling Reformed congregations of Pennsylvania, and for a brief period preached
at Rhinebeck, N. Y. Reiger arrived in this country in
September, 1731. He settled at Lancaster, and supplied
the surrounding congregations with preaching, namely,
Conestoga, Schaefferstown, etc. These three men have
a number of things in common, viz., 1, they united in
September 29, 1747, with the Rev. Mr. Schlatter in the
establishment, in Philadelphia, of the first ecclesiastical
organization, known then by the name of Cœtus, now
as Synod; 2, they founded the first churches in the
localities where they settled; 3, they all accumulated
considerable wealth; 4, they all lie buried in the churches
which they respectively founded; and 5, they were all
among the first supplies of the Tulpehocken congregation. Would we visit their respective graves, we should
find Weiss buried at the south-east corner of the New
Goschenhoppen church, the grave marked by a wooden
slab on which is painted the barest fact of his resting
there. While he died childless, he owned about twenty
slaves, all of whom and their offspring he baptized,

some of whose descendants still linger about Goschen-hoppen. The grave of Boehm is likewise in the southeast corner of the church he built at Whitpain, having died suddenly, May 1, 1749, after a trip to Egypt, Lehigh county, where on the previous day he had administered the communion to that flock. He left a number of children, among whom was long preserved, as a relic, an iron chest filled with this pioneer's most important church papers and correspondence with the church judicatories of Holland and Germany, but which valuable historic treasures were, after oft handling, finally but most unfortunately given to the flames. Reiger lies buried in the First Reformed church of Lancaster, a horizontal stone, with an elaborate epitaph, marking the spot, and noting his death as occurring in 1769, March the 11th.

When the Rev. Michael Schlatter, the great leader and organizer of the German Reformed church of America (sent by the Reformed Classes of Holland, and commissioned to consolidate the scattered Reformed congregations upon the basis of their denominational order, doctrines and worship) arrived in this country, these three named pastors at one time accompanied him to this congregation at the Tulpehocken. The illustrious patriarch visited here on several other occasions, but perhaps the most memorable visit of all is that occasioned by the introduction and installation of the first regular pastor, in the person of the Rev. Dominicus Bartholomaeus, whom, with Rev. Hochrentuer, he was instrumental in inducing to come to America from Switzerland for the important fields at Tulpehocken and Lancaster, respectively.

Rev. Bartholomaeus took charge at Tulpehocken, September, 1748, but was not permitted to labor for any length of time. Almost from the very beginning of his ministry his health was precarious, causing him to cease from its active labors here in 1752, and being relieved of his bodily infirmities by death in 1759. The writer does not know his place of burial. Rev. Dr. William Stoy, who succeeded this first pastor at Tulpehocken, was born in Herborn, Germany, March 14, 1726, where he was educated for the ministry, and accompanied Rev. Mr. Schlatter to America, one of six pastors, whom this leader induced, in a visit to the Fatherland in 1752, to accompany him to America to serve the church here. He was appointed as successor to Mr. Bartholomaeus, when failing health debilitated the latter. He remained but three years, when the severity of the climate induced him to resign. After health improved he accepted a call to Lancaster, and from thence came back to the Lebanon Valley, settling in Lebanon and operating up and down this valley as a physician and minister. He preached here and at Host church in Berks county for some time longer, at which latter place he was buried, according to his own ante-mortem request. A memorial stone with suitable inscription marks his resting place. He died in Lebanon, September 14, 1801. Whatever may have been the influence of his gospel teachings, his medical skill was admitted, and from his saddle-bags he oft took cures for the body. We know not the result of his offers of the water of eternal life. Among his remedies was a popular preparation known as "Stoy's Drops" and an effectual cure for hydrophobia.

Rev. John Waldschmidt, who served Tulpehocken from 1757 to 1758, was also a native of Germany, and one of the six pastors whom Mr. Schlatter induced to labor in the American field. He was first stationed in Lancaster county, and from thence supplied this church for nearly two years. He died in September, 1786, and lies buried in the Swamp (Lancaster county) church yard, a stone fittingly inscribed marking the spot.

Rev. Wm. Otterbein, another German, succeeded Mr. Waldschmidt in this charge in 1758. He likewise was one of Rev. Mr. Schlatter's six apostles, induced by his appeal to leave home and native land in the interests of the Reformed Zion in America. He, with the other five, was ordained to the gospel ministry at the Hague and accompanied their earnest leader across the mighty deep in 1752. He was a youth of 26 when he arrived, and at once entered into an agreement with the Lancaster congregation to serve them for five years. He established order and discipline in the church, introducing the time-honored custom of each communicant's personal interview with the pastor (*Anmeldung*) a day or two prior to the communion. The original paper, drawn up by him and signed by 80 members of his flock, is preserved in the archives of the Lancaster church. He was successful in giving strength and stability to this congregation—inducing them to erect during his ministry a massive stone church edifice, which stood almost a century before it was displaced by the present brick structure. He resigned in 1758 and assumed charge at Tulpehocken, only as temporary supply at first, which continued, however, for several years. From Tulpehocken Mr. Otterbein went to Frederick, Md., and from thence to Baltimore. Here he labored for almost 40 years, until his death, being, however, meanwhile instrumental in giving form and shape to a new sect or denomination, the United Brethren in Christ. Later he seems to have come back to his first love, taking a deep interest in the Reformed church and dying within her fold, one of the most highly gifted preachers and intensely ardent workers ot this denomination. He died October 17, 1813, in Baltimore, where the venerable Dr. Kurtz, of the Lutheran church, ministered to him in his dying hours and preached his German funeral sermon. He lies buried near the then Reformed church, now United Brethren, in Conway street of that city. Bishop Asbury, first bishop of the M. E. church, whom the former assisted to consecrate to the bishopric, and whose intimate friendship he enjoyed, spoke a special eulogium to his memory in the Conway street church from Rev. iii. 10-11. Mr. Otterbein's tomb is well preserved and marked by a marble entablature, bearing the data of a brief memorial.

Rev. John J. Zufall succeeded Mr. Otterbein at Tulpehocken, and served this charge from 1765 to 1769. There is not much recorded concerning this pastor's work or career from which the writer could trace a life sketch.

Rev. William Hendel, Sr., served Tulpehocken from 1769 to 1782. He arrived in this country from his native Palatinate in 1764, and assumed charge at Lancaster. From thence he came to Tulpehocken, laboring here during the Revolutionary war period. After an efficient ministry of thirteen years, he returned to Lancaster. In 1794, he accepted a call to Philadelphia, laboring there during that period of trial occasioned by the pestilence, which plague finally made him its victim, ending in death September 28, 1798. He is buried by the side of many of his ministerial brethren, in Franklin Square, Philadelphia. Dr. Helmuth, of the Lutheran church, his warm and faithful friend, preached at his obsequies, from the text 2 Samuel i. 26. Dr. Harbaugh called Hendel "the St. John of the Reformed Church." A friend composed a special hymn on his death, which, however, we have not space to quote.

Rev. Andrew Loretz, the next pastor, was a sort of unaccountable personage in the annals of the Reformed Church—a mysterious, Melchizedek kind of prophet, whose parentage and general history is hidden. A native of Switzerland, he came to America in 1784, and the next year settled at Tulpehocken, where he served this church and those at Swatara, Heidelbergtown, Lebanon and Hill. His Swiss dialect is said to have interfered with his usefulness here, and he, therefore, soon returned to Europe, leaving this charge again vacant in 1786.

Rev. Daniel Wagner succeeded him in 1787. He was born in the duchy of Nassau, Germany, but came with his parents to this country when two years of age, settling temporarily in Chester county, but after a few years taking up their permanent abode in Bern township, Berks county, Pa. He labored in the ministry in York county for fifteen years before assuming charge at Tulpehocken, where he remained four years, when he again returned to York, remaining nine years longer, when he settled at Frederick, Md. After a few more years' labor here he became disabled, removing back to York in 1810, only to die and be buried there, which occurred in December of the same year. There many of his descendants still reside.

Rev. Dr. Wm. Hendel, Jr., eldest son of the senior Hendel, succeeded Rev. Wagner. In youth he was under the tutelage of the celebrated Lutheran divines, Drs. Kunze and Helmuth, graduating later from Columbia college, N. Y., and from the New Brunswick Theological Seminary. He was ordained in 1793, and at once assumed charge at Tulpehocken, remaining thirty years. He was a progressive man, much in advance of his brethren of that day in point of liberal thought. For his advocacy of missions and the establishment of a

Theological Seminary of his church he was violently persecuted. It was by his casting vote, as President of Synod, that the first Theological Seminary of the Reformed church was established. In 1823 he resigned several of his churches and removed to Womelsdorf, where he continued to preach six years longer, when he retired from the sacred office, only preaching occasionally after that date as supply for his brethren. He died at Womelsdorf on July 11, 1846, and there was buried. (See chapter on Womelsdorf.)

At his funeral the Rev. John C. Bucher, of Reading, who was one of the officiating clergymen, made the startling statement at the request of deceased, that he (the deceased) had lived and preached all his years with a mere theoretical knowledge of the religion and the grace of God, and that he had never enjoyed the favor and pardon of God in its fullest and experimental sense before impending death opened his eyes to his dreadful situation. He then called on God and found peace. By request, this statement was to be made at his funeral, to warn other pastors against a false trust or hope, and to urge his own members to seek the Lord's pardon and experimental grace while it was yet day. The "Evangelical Association," or some members of it, made stock of this confession, and gave it publicity by means of a printed tract which they circulated.

The Leinbach brethren, Thomas and Charles, in turn succeeded Dr. Hendel at Tulpehocken, and served the charge for more than fifty years. They were both well adapted for this field, and under the ministry of the former some of the greatest improvements of the church were made—such as the building of the present church edifice, and the celebration of the centennial of the church in 1847, all of which helped to strengthen the cause of the congregation. He also succeeded in dividing the large membership into two congregations, and thus establishing the Reformed congregation at Myerstown, and building that edifice. He died at Millersburg, Berks county, on Thursday, March 31, 1864, having there been seized with violent sickness, while officiating on the preceding Sunday. His funeral was a solemn occasion, attended by a large concourse of people, when several sermons were preached, the principal one by Dr. J. S. Dubbs, of Allentown, who was a classmate of his, and a mutual friend throughout life— each having officiated at the marriage of the other. Mr. Leinbach was the first person buried in the new cemetery at Tulpehocken, and a marble monument marks the site of his resting place, close to its entrance near the church. The following inscription is engraved thereon :

In Memory of
Rev. Thomas H. Leinbach,
Pastor of this Con-
gregation for 38 years.
Commenced
in March, 1826,
Ended
in March, 1864.
"I am the Resurrection and the Life, &c."

His brother Charles succeeded him, and served the church for 20 years. He lies buried near his brother, and a granite shaft tells this story:

REV. CHARLES H. LEINBACH, D. D.,
Born
Nov. 7, 1815.
Died
July 15, 1883.
"He Giveth His Beloved Sleep."
Pastor Tulpehocken Charge, May 1, 1863, to July, 1883.

Since 1884 Pastor Welker has done good work here, and continues his successful labors. But we cannot tarry any longer. Therefore, dismissing this distinguished array of divines, and breaking up our happy conference with the living and dead abruptly, let us be off after the many landmarks that still abide in this historically rich valley. To the departed, "*Requiescant in pace!*" To the only living pastoral toiler and his helpers, "*Dominus Vobiscum!*"

CHAPTER XVI.

THE genial spring sun has made angling seasonable. The very allusion to this boyhood sport, combines with the climate to awaken fondest memories. A flood of delightful recollections, like unto the brooks at spring-time, all whose fountain-heads have been let loose and whose banks run full to overflowing, is started and flows through the channels of our soul at the very sight of a stream of water in spring time. Being on the banks of a gamey stream, how would it be if we'd spend a day in fishing up the historic Tulpehocken? All my readers being agreed, this will we do to-day. Only we shall not angle for the finny tribe, but will endeavor to land a few big fish in the line of facts of antique interest, that sport unknown or almost forgotten in the stream of historic events that courses along the banks of this familiar creek.

Therefore, leaving the comfortable and ancient old manse of the Reformed by the Tulpehocken, we will go up its waters, along which our forefathers made the first settlement in this valley. First, then, we come to the old mill. property, known for over a century as the "Church Mill," because until recently it was owned by the congregation and turned out one grist for the temporal support of the church and another to furnish the supporting staff of the temporal life of its membership. Thence, going up the windings of this stream, there is not an old homestead from here to its source, five miles west, that has not a story of earnest struggle and anxious fear, because of the many depredations of the savages, hid away in its early history. Here the land was first occupied by the earliest settlers, because of the water convenience. Here the Schoharie fugitives first squatted and developed their plantations, for which most of them afterwards paid. Along this stream, the Millbach and the Swatara, the very first homes in the valley were founded. Many of these homesteads have come into other hands, but until recently many were still in the possession of the direct descendants of the original owners.

If we would take our stroll up the turnpike, just a quarter of a mile at most places north of this creek, and running in the main parallel to it, we could the better point out these old settlements, because this excellent highway is on higher ground. And thither let us repair to gain the best point of view. Our line—a line of vision, however—will still be long enough to let the baited hook drop into this stream to our south, and also into the "Owl Creek," that rises in the hillsides to our north and flows in a westerly and southwesterly course, emptying into the Tulpehocken just east of Myerstown.

Along the Tulpehocken are the Haack and Kreitzer

and Briddebach (Breitenbach) estates and others. Along the Owl creek are the homesteads of the original Anspachs, Walborns, Lauers, Noackres, Lenne, and so forth. The whole of this territory to the north and south, and even more than is included in this described district, lying east of Myerstown, situated in what is now Jackson township, was originally taken up by one Casper Wister, who is described in all ancient documents as "the brass-button maker of Philadelphia." The writer was recently shown, by the present owner of the Breitenbach farm, Mr. Richard Miller, of Myerstown, an old parchment deed, dated August 7, 1754, which legally conveyed the small tract of about four acres from Martin Noacker and wife to Philip Breitenbach, for the sum of 35 pounds, 8 shillings and 6 pence. Said tract was a portion of a farm which Martin Noacker bought of John Noacker in 1750, who had purchased it from Casper Wister, "the brass-button maker of Philadelphia," who had received, November 10, 1738, by indenture from the proprietaries, the amount of 1,724 acres, at an annual quit rental of one red rose for 10,000 acres. On this four-acre tract an Indian fort was erected by Philip Breitenbach, to which the neighboring inhabitants were wont to flee in cases of emergency during the war period with the Indians. We are told that the great-hearted Breitenbach "was wont, on many occasions of alarm, to take his drum and beat it on an eminence near his house, to collect the neighbors from work, into the fort. On one occasion the Indians

pursued them close to the house, when one of the inmates took up a gun and shot the Indian dead on the
spot."—*Rupp's History of Berks and Lebanon Counties.*

On this "eminence" of Breitenbach, evidently east
of his home, where we find it as of old, let us take our
stand and "view the landscape o'er." We are just half
a mile east of Myerstown. Our feet now rest on truly

THE BREITENBACH INDIAN FORT HOMESTEAD, EAST OF MYERSTOWN.

historic ground. Facing the west, before us lies the
Breitenbach homestead, on the south of the pike. The
headstone on barn (second building) bears date of 1802.
By it, at the base of the brow of this historic "emi-

nence," flows the "Owl Creek," in which, tradition says, General Washington watered his horse on one of his visits to or journeys through this valley. To the left, but a little over a stone's throw from the pike, stands an old stone residence, with arched cellar, seventeen steps deep, for safe refuge from the savages, which may be the Indian fort which Breitenbach built, though another spot near the Owl creek is pointed out as the place where, until recently, the ruins could be seen. This old relic, still standing, but fast going into decay because no longer occupied, is now the property of Mr. Harry Kreitzer, of Philadelphia, who, just a little east of our observation point, has a comfortable residence for his summer quarters. Near this place, on the Kreitzer estate, is the stone crusher—long since idle, after a futile attempt at gold mining. To our right, on the north side of the pike, almost near enough to touch the roofs of the buildings, is the present Tice homestead, but for a long time used as a hotel, and built by Peter Len, in 1777. It is a large and well-kept limestone country house, surrounded by ample grounds as yard. A special stone in the side of the house facing the roadway, bears the somewhat common legend found on old homes in this district, namely:

```
    GOTT . GESEGNE . DIE-
    SES . HAVS . WER DA GET
    EIN . VND . AVS . 1777.
    PETR . LEN . EFA LENIN
```

As a door-step, a broken milestone has done service for many years. It bears the following information to the wayfarer that may chance to try the knocker of this hospitable home, and who casts his eyes downward while awaiting a response:

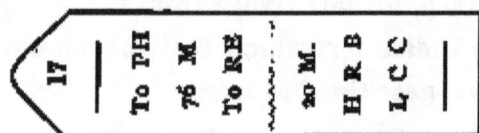

```
17 |  To PH   M   To RE  :  20 M.   H R B   L C C  |
        76
```

Over this door-step have walked the Tice family, as they took leave of the old home—some of whom have since gone out to their long home. One son has used it as a stepping-stone from a peaceful and quiet home-life into the prominence and usefulness of a professor's life, and is now employed in some institution in Montgomery county.

A little north of the Tice homestead is the Noacker farm, with its imposing farm dwellings, settled early, as we have already seen, on a portion of the "brass-button maker's" tract.   Beyond this place is the Lauer home, where the greatest benefactor (?) to the bibulous of old Berks and of East Pennsylvania generally, was reared—the noted beer-brewer of Reading, Mr. Frederick Lauer.

Between the Tice homestead and the Noacker farm, the grading of the land still shows where the old road wound around the steep "eminence" of Breitenbach, before the Berks and Dauphin turnpike was located right over it. It crossed the Owl creek at about the same place the pike does, and took a westerly and southwesterly course from thence to the Tulpehocken, south of Myerstown, where still stands the residence of this town's founder, Mr. Isaac Myers.

And right here, in front of the old Breitenbach home, where this pioneer parted this life, we will part company for the day. Let me only add that Mr. and Mrs. Breitenbach lie buried side by side on the Christ Tulpehocken Lutheran graveyard, and their graves are marked by fitting stones. The following is a specimen of their tombstones, the wife's (Elizabeth) being similar to his:

Hier Ruhet
PHILIP BREITENBACH
War gebohren
den 6 October 1725
und starb
den 26 October 1790
War alt
65 Jahr und 20 Tage.

CHAPTER XVII.

TULPEHOCKENTOWN, ALIAS MYERSTOWN.

IT may not be generally known, even to the inhabitants of the town itself, that Myerstown—the place we are about to "do" historically to-day—was originally called Tulpehockentown. It is a question whether all the Lebanon county towns had not better kept their first names and thus carried out the evident wishes of their modest founders, who stood as sponsors when these local communities were originally christened. There certainly seems more beauty and taste in such names as Newburg, Heidelbergtown, Nassau, Williamsburg and Tulpehockentown, than such bold appellations of ownership as a later generation attributed and expressed in the present sobriquets of Newmanstown, Schaefferstown, Stumpstown, Jonestown, and Myerstown. Lebanon has done wisely in dropping the assumed name of its founder and adopting instead the euphonious Scriptural name first given to the township in which it was located. Think of such a city as Lebanon being called by the German jawbreaker, *Steitztown!*

But what is there in a name? Well, in the instance of most of our country towns, it preserves a fact in the history of their founding. And since they teach us his-

(156)

tory, we shall let them stand. Only what I have to say concerning first names is history also, and therefore I insist on being heard when I recall to the minds of my readers what is evinced from old documents, that the original name given to Myerstown was Tulpehockentown. It does not require any extensive search, or any stretch of the imagination, to find a reason for this. The town was located on the banks of this stream, close to which stood, and still stands, the house of its founder, Mr. Isaac Myers. Let me therefore lead my readers to this landmark, from which to take bearings.

Leaving the Breitenbach "eminence," just east of town, the old road was identical with the pike, from the east about a square into town, from whence its course branched off this present main thoroughfare of the borough to the southwest, till it reached the Tulpehocken, at where the Myers residence is still found, about a quarter of a mile due south of the town center. There is an old log house—now encased in weatherboards—that still stands at this junction of the pike with the old road, which faced this original highway and stands therefore at an angle to the pike, which it also attempts to front. When Isaac Myers in 1768 laid out the village, this old highway still led through a dense forest, and within it were planted, as the first scattered homes of the new settlement, the houses of Christian Maurer, Henry Brill, Nicolas Gast, Messrs. Haussegger, Schumacher, Hoffman, Schnell, etc., most of them honest German artisans. As early as 1738 a tract of

321 acres was conveyed by "the brass-button maker of
Philadelphia" (Casper Wister), to Henry Bassler, whose
descendants of the fifth generation still "hold the fort"
in the western end of town. This family has been

THE ISAAC MEIER HOMESTEAD, MYERSTOWN.

prominent in the annals of the town. The grandfather
of the present John H. Bassler, who attained a reputation for brilliant services in the late rebellion, Simon
Bassler, Sr., "was detailed as one of the company called
upon to guard the captured Hessians imprisoned for a
time at Hebron."

Mr. Isaac Myers, the founder, was a native of this valley. He built his home on the banks of the Tulpehocken

about the middle of last century. Here he reared his family, some of whose descendants have made their mark in life. Among them are such names as the Hiesters and Reilys and Woods—families into which his daughters were married. Both Captain John Reily and Col. Joseph Wood, two sons-in-law, achieved notoriety during the revolution. The late Prof. Wm. M. Reily, Ph. D., long at the head of Palatinate College* (Reformed) located here, was a descendant.

The old house has passed out of the family hand and name, and is now the property of Dr. W. C. Kline, the enterprising druggist of town. It is quite a relic of antiquity. Its walls are three feet thick, it having often sheltered the neighbors from the attacks of the Indians. The present owner has carefully kept in their original condition the garret rooms, which were once occupied by the colored slaves of its first, likewise their owner and master.

The manner in which so conspicuous and enterprising a career as that of the founder of Myerstown came to an end is worthy of note. Being elected to the office of magistrate, there were public acts of his to be performed which incurred the enmity of some persons. Hence a snare was set for taking vengeance on him. Being summoned away from home one night on the ostensible purpose of transacting business at some wayside inn, Mr. Myers answered the call, and here fell a victim into the

---

* This school is now (1895) the Albright Collegiate Institute of the United Evangelical Church.

hands of his secret foes. Sitting with his back to a
window, he was fatally shot from the outside. He lived
long enough to be taken to his home, however, whither
he summoned a few friends with whom he held an
interview, after which he requested his wife never to
search for his murderers nor prosecute them if discovered,
as their guilty conscience would be punishment enough
for them. He then died in the bosom of his family.
We found his grave in the old Tulpehocken Reformed
graveyard marked by a large, flat stone, about 2½ by 6
ft., covering his entire grave. The following inscription is still quite legible :

HIER LIGT IN
GOTT SELICH
ENTSCHLAFEN
ISACK . MEIER
IST GEBOHREN
1730 DE 4TE
IANVARI. IST
GESTORBEN
1770 DEN 5TE
IVLI. SO WAR
SEIN GANZES
ALTER 40 IA-
HR. V. 6 MONAT
SEIN LEIGEN
TEXT STET
IN DER ERSTEN
EPL. PETRI
IM 5TE C H.
IM 8. V. 9. VE.

Dr. Kline is also the owner and occupant of another noted landmark of this town.   This is the residence of the late Governor J. Andreas Shultze.   It is a well known fact that after this illustrious son of the pious

THE SHULTZE HOUSE, MYERSTOWN.

Lutheran pastor at Tulpehocken had himself studied for the ministry and made an attempt of its arduous labors, finding himself physicially incapacitated for its trials and hardships in that day, relinquished the sacred calling and entered secular life.   He settled in Myerstown, and for a number of years carried on the mercantile business here.   This place is somewhat centrally located

on the north side of its main street. It has been used
for the past sixteen years as the site of the town postoffice,
and only abandoned as such recently at a change of the
complexion of our National administration.   Since 1879
this old store stand and home has been the property of
Dr. Kline, whose family occupies the domestic portion
of the historic edifice, while the doctor's drug-store fills
the newer portion of the building, not used by the postoffice, which latter is a room of about 30 by 25 feet in
dimensions, now vacant since the ex-postmaster, Mr.
Milton Myers, was obliged to hand his keys and commission over to his Democratic successor.   The stone
barn erected on the rear of the lot still bears the date of
its erection and the initials of the once illustrious owner
and dweller here, through whose veins flowed at successive stages of his life the blood of theology, business
and statesmanship.   The following is a fac-simile of
this date stone:

J. A. S.

1808

It would seem as if ownership or occupancy of this
Shultze house brought distinction in its course, for there
has not been a possessor of it since, who has not grown

into some degree of local fame. From Shultze the property passed into the hands of Daniel Stine, esq., who was afterwards elected to the legislature. He transferred it to Mr. Joseph Coover, who! was elected associate judge of the county in 1866. So likewise it was owned by Mr. Burkholder, who attained some prominence; and by W. M. Ulrich, who rose in the rebellion to the distinction of General, and who has since the late war founded an independent settlement in Virginia, about 20 miles south of Washington, D. C., which he has named "Mt. Herndon," and where he resides in affluence and honor. The writer gives this timely notice to the present owner to prepare himself for the "lightning" of greatness which has been accustomed to take this old building as a favorite conductor. "Some men are born great, some achieve greatness, but some have greatness thrust upon them."

By going a few hundred yards to the west of this Shultze house, we come to the spot where until recently stood, to the south of the pike or main street, an old landmark of historic interest. This was the old school house of ante-revolutionary founding. The site is now occupied by a modern frame house owned by a Mrs. Dundore. The writer was recently shown a parchment deed by ex-Judge Coover, dated Sept. 12, 1765, wherein Simon Bassler and his wife, Eva Maria, conveyed to Nicholas Swingle, jr., and Nicholas Hauseker, trustees, a certain tract of land or lot described as bordering on lands of Isaac Myers, &c., for the sum of one pound

and 10 shillings for school purposes forever. This was
acknowledged before the noted J. P. DeHaas, esq., and
recorded at Lancaster by Edward Shippen, recorder.
On this lot a school house was erected, which was as a
"city set on a hill" to enlighten four or five generations
of Myerstown's young Americans. When finally these
subscription or parochial schools were superseded by
our free schools, this old friend gradually grew into dis-
favor until the building alone was left to tell its story of
former blessedness. When Mr. Daniel Stine represented
this district in our state legislature he was authorized
by an act of assembly to vacate or sell the property and
with the money to buy a burial ground, where the community for "six miles around" might find the right of
sepulture, Messrs. Bassler and Mosser being trustees.
In this deed, to which are affixed quaint seals, the town
is named "Tulpehockiutown."

Another old school house, octagonal in shape, still
stands at the eastern end of town, but is now used as a
blacksmith shop.

On the old cemetery (Lutheran and Reformed) located
in the western portion of the town, next to the Frieden's
Lutheran church, are found the graves of the old sires
and settlers of this community. Such names as the
Leys, Valentines, Spanglers, Batdorfs, Grohs, Mossers,
Stoevers, Burkholders, Koppenhavers, Basslers, Zart-
mans, etc., are among the oldest. Close to the church
walls are two graves that meant more to me than others,
because here we know stood the ex-Governor Shultze

when their enclosed remains were solemnly laid aside. They are the graves of Mr. and Mrs. Leonard Immel, the parents-in-law of this noted governor. The following epitaph marks the resting place of this sturdy illustrious farmer, whose rural home to the southwest of town the young, ambitious preacher-merchant entered to carry away as prize an accomplished and winsome daughter:

Denckmal
Der Liebe Fur
LEONHARD IMMEL
Sohn von
Johann und Barbara Immel.
Er erblickte das Licht dieser Welt auf
den 14ten Tag October 1747
und starb
den 2ten Tag Juny A. D. 1839.
Brachte seine irdische Walfarth auf
91 Jahre, 7 Monate
und 20 Tag.
——
Leichentext die 2 Epistle St. Pauli an
Timotheum, das 4 Capital,
Der 7 u 8 vers.

The wife's tombstone is similar in form and its inscription akin in substance to his. And here where these illustrious kindred parted company for life we will end this chapter.

CHAPTER XVIII.

A WALK OVER HISTORIC GROUND.

HAVING parted company with my readers in the shadow of the Myerstown Lutheran and Reformed churches, which lift up their tall spires towards the skies as memorials of the piety of the generations that have passed away, as constant indices pointing to and reminding one of a protecting and beneficient divine Ruler, and as so many marks of grace and ornament to the thriving borough that has spread itself about their base, let us prepare to take a walk to-day of several miles up the pike, which leads through truly historic ground. Casting our eyes to the north and south—especially to the south, where flows the story-laden Tulpehocken—we shall pass not a single old homestead that is not linked by a chainwork of interesting events to the earliest days of this valley's settlement.

Before leaving, however, this long-time meeting place of these honored German ancestors and this final gathering place of their bones, where most of the illustrious sires sleep, whose once thriving homes we shall visit to-day, let us take a brief look into the history of these churches. Thus we learn that originally this locality worshipped at the Tulpehocken churches, as few others besides Lutherans and Reformed had settled here. In course of time, however, distance and the increase of population in this vicinity suggested the planting of churches at Myerstown. Accordingly as early as 1811, steps were taken towards organizing the Lutheran church by the westernmost members of the Tulpehocken flock. At the original meeting, held June 23, 1811, it was resolved to build a church, and as a building committee the following persons were chosen, viz.: Christian Ley, Leonard Immel, Leonard Rambler, Jacob Laehn, Christopher Liess, Christian Artz and Martin Moyer. We have already learned that Messrs. Michael Mosser and Simon Bassler donated a lot for building and burial purposes—the latter common to Lutherans and Reformed alike—to all "living within a radius of six miles." All of these leaders named lie buried on this ancient graveyard, and into most of their homes we shall have occasion to peep to-day. The first trustees were Michael Ley, Leonard Immel and J. Andreas Shulze, the future governor.

In 1812 the church was built and consecrated. It was a stone structure, and was of sufficient dimensions for the time (55x36 ft.,) and at once equipped with a bell and soon with a pipe organ. In 1857 the present imposing brick edifice was erected. The following pastors have served the same:

Rev. William Baetes 1812-1824
Rev. W. G. Ernst, D. D. 1824-1849
Rev. G. F. Krotel, D. D. 1849-1852

The Reformed did not withdraw from the mother (Tulpehocken) church until 1860, when 250 members, who had been for some time previously served as a branch congregation, separated and organized the church and erected the large and commodious limestone structure now gracing this end of town. The Mossers, Diehls, Basslers, Sherks, Looses, Spanglers, Muths, Baneys, Tices and others have been the leading families of this flock, now about 500 strong. Only Rev. Dr. George Wolff and his son, David, have preceded the present pastor, Rev. Mr. Gonser, in the sacred office here. The latter assumed the charge only about two years ago.

There are other churches of town, such as the United Brethren and the Evangelical, which have doubtless exerted their healthful influence upon the community, but they do not stand so much in the line of the ancient and the historic, and therefore we shall not enter into their records, but bid this ancient "Tulpehockentown" a reluctant good-bye, and begin our march up the valley to where many of the earliest noted actors of this community first planted their American homes.

Turning to the south from West Myerstown, the first plantation west of Myers' is that of Heinrich Bassler, who in 1738 purchased of "the brass-button maker of Philadelphia" a tract of over 300 acres and reared his home on the banks of the Tulpehocken. Here he raised a family that has continued to this day of the fifth or sixth generation to hand down the mantle of this pioneer's energy and far-sightedness. These have kept the name untarnished, some of them adding to its celebrity for valor and patriotism. They have also kept the old homestead in the family name and hands. The present owner is Mrs. Sallie Bassler.

The next western neighbor, settled even before Mr. Bassler and also on the Tulpehocken, was Leonhard Ramler. The original buildings have all been superseded by second buildings, though these are quite old. The present owner is Mr. John Gockley. There hangs about this place the story, so common throughout this valley, of shelter against Indian depredations. All along this valley, in truth, the tomahawk and scalping knife were used. (It should have been said in connection with the first long-historic German school-house of Myerstown, that tradition reports the massacre of seven white persons there ·by the Indians.) From this home wended the first funeral procession to the Myerstown cemetery, when Mrs. Anna Barbara Ramler, at the age of 78 years, was borne hence for burial there.

Going still westward along the banks of this stream, we come next to the Immel homestead, originally one plantation, but later subdivided into two farms. The easternmost house, which may have been the first, so inferred on account of traces of an old road near it and the story of fortifications here, has yielded to the exac-

tions of time, and been displaced about twenty-two
years ago by a new structure of frame.   It is now owned
by the Donges Bros. of the Myerstown mercantile firm,
and the farm is in present charge of Mr. Dechert.   But
the westernmost homestead is quite ancient.   It has all

THE IMMEL HOMESTEAD.

the characteristics of age, such as its broken front door,
its wall closets, its fifteen-inch wide oak flooring, its
large and wide Queen Anne mantel and fire place, and
its solid masonry, well preserved.   Only the tiles have
given place to shingles, the former stored beside the
home, which if they were old-fashioned German waffles
—a thing they much resemble—should have been de-

voured long ago. We should think they would "take"
as relics among the descendants of the Immels and
Governor Shulze, quite as well as such hot-cakes. For
here it was that the future Governor of our State visited
when a youth, and in his best suit and smiles.

There was a charming daughter in this home in his
day, then presided over by Leonhard Immel, who had
completely captivated this young aspirant's heart. Was
she a member of his father's choir at Tulpehocken,
famous and enchanting for her singing, or only a meek
and modest member of the flock, winsome for her piety
or her blushing beauty? The writer cannot tell. But
the charm went forth from her life that landed Cupid's
dart, and left it quivering in the heart of the pastor's
noble son, which made him doubtless repair once a week
to this ancient fireside for healing. We took interest in
finding the identical room in which this courtship was
held, unchanged by any modernization whatever. The
interior arrangement of this house might well serve as a
model, so well is the space utilized. The stairway is
convenient to every apartment and yet out of the way.
The rooms communicate and are accessible from the
hall, in which is a large fire-place and Queen Anne
oak mantel, that speaks of the charms and poetry of
rural life in winter. The farm is now the property
of Mrs. Capt. John H. Bassler, a sister of Rev. Dr.
Mosser, of Reading. The following inscription we
found on a sandstone still preserved in the front elevation:

HANNES
IMMEL
ANNA
BARBARA.

17   50

This "Hannes Immel" was the father of Leonhard
Immel, whose name has already been alluded to and his
tombstone transcribed in our last chapter, who was the
father of Mrs. Gov. Shulze, and the progenitor of the
Immels still found in this community, one of whom fills
the honorable position of banker at Myerstown. Mr.
Zartman is farming the plantation where these illustrious
ancestors raised their earlier crops.

Next west to Immels is the Spangler home. This
original homestead is now also divided into two farms.
The westernmost home is the site of the first dwellings,
and those now standing are considerably over a century
old. The barn contains a stone bearing date of 1782,
with initials of "G. Sp." and "B. Sp." This farm is
now owned by Miss Cora Kilmer, while the east half is
the property of Mr. Henry Hauck.

Next we come to the most historic and wealthy ancient homestead of them all. It is the reputed Ley (Lei) homestead and is located at the source of the Tulpehocken, about two miles west of Myerstown. Here from among limestone rocks springs forth the Tulpe-

THE ANCIENT LEI (LEY) HOMESTEAD, MODERNIZED BY MR. SAMUEL URICH, (PRESENT OWNER).

hocken, like Minerva from the head of Jove, a full-grown stream and daughter of the mighty deep. Here the Indians had reared a village of wigwams and buried their dead, many of whose bones and relics have been disinterred during the making of recent excavations.

Here the wealthy German emigrant Lei pitched his tent and took up 1000 acres of land. In 1769 he, or his son, built the second house which is still standing, remodeled and enlarged by its present owner, Mr. Samuel Urich, into one of the most palatial abodes of the county. But even in the days of its erection it was already a mansion. It has a lovely site on a hillock fronting the south. Its walls, now ivy-covered in part, are of regular dressed limestone, with sandstone trimmings. Two sandstones in its front elevation read as follows :

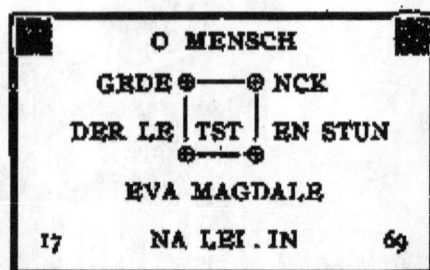

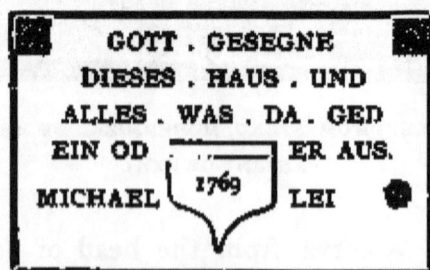

O MENSCH
GEDE ●——● NCK
DER LE | TST | EN STUN
EVA MAGDALE
17   NA LEI . IN   69

GOTT . GESEGNE
DIESES . HAUS . UND
ALLES . WAS . DA . GED
EIN OD ┌───┐ ER AUS.
MICHAEL 1769 LEI

Hither General Washington came with some of his staff officers, such as Generals Hiester, Keim and Ermentrout of Berks county, and others, for a few days' hunt and recreation. It is supposed this happened in 1777, when Washington's army occupied Valley Forge, inasmuch as a letter extant—addressed by Washington to Gen. Wayne, from Reading Furnace, September 17, 1777—shows him to have been in this valley then. It may also have been in November, 1793, when President of the United States, inasmuch as he spent the night of the 13th of that month and year in Womelsdorf, where the Ermentrouts then lived. Tradition has the following story of this visit. One day about half a dozen riders reined up their horses in front of this hospitable abode, then still comparatively surrounded by a forest. It chanced that Mrs. Lei and a "redemptioner" woman by the name of Sherk—ancestor of the present Sherk family of this valley—who served here, were washing clothes at the wash-house in their bare feet and scant loose habits. Their attention was called by these strange yeomanry-soldiers amid great embarrassment and confusion. The strangers presently made known their names and purposes, whereupon the men folks were summoned from the fields, who soon responded to speak and act the words and deeds of welcome. Soon plans were consummated for a two or three days' fishing and hunting sport, for all of which the guests were prepared and the host was soon ready. In the southwest room, known as the Blue Room, of this ancient hospitable abode, the host, who was a Revolutionary Captain, spent the evenings with his illustrious visitors, while the southeast room on the second floor is still pointed out as the bed-room of the great General. This latter was always the private sleeping room of the late Rev. Isaac K. Loose, of Bethlehem, when he visited his old home, the property having fallen into the Loose hands after it slipped out of those of this original owner and his descendants, which occurred through heavy losses in coal speculation in the time of Christian, a son or grandson. Many other noteworthy incidents cluster about this place which would be interesting to the average reader, but space forbids their mention.

Both the original Michael and Eva M. Lei are buried at the Union graveyard at Myerstown, in the shadow of Frieden's Lutheran church, herein described. He died in 1824 (born 1739), and she in 1815 (born 1744). Here also lies buried their son Christian, who was born in 1762 and died in 1832, having been, as we have seen, a member of the building committee of the church. His wife, Anna Catharine (Coppenhoffer), died by accidental poisoning January 11th, 1822, and lies buried by his side. Their son, Christian, died a few years ago at Pinegrove, a nonegenarian.

But we must go on in our westward march. By going a mile up the pike from this place and turning north an eighth of a mile at Mr. Cyrus Baney's palatial residence, we will reach the farm of Mr. Henry Tice of West Myerstown. There are stones in the large house showing that it was erected by Philip and Eve Tice in 1821, who were descendants of the first settlers here, whose original house contains an anvil-shaped stone in its gable, reading thus:

M. T.

1744.

This is the house from which was taken the richly-finished walnut door now on exhibition in Mr. George M. Stanley's store of Lebanon. It consists of 356 pieces, inlaid and carved. Not a nail is used in its construction. Here it swung on its curious wrought-iron hinges for a century and a half, letting in and out successive generations of Tices... We will let an imaginary swing of this door bring to an abrupt close the wanderings over historic territory we have taken in this chapter.

CHAPTER XIX.

FOR the past four months I have conducted my army of explorers through the historic field lying east of Lebanon, and have been making constant approaches towards this desired haven. In these weekly marches I have taken my army, like Coxey did his, through slush and snow. But as Coxey finally ended his notorious march towards Washington by his arrival in the Nation's capitol, so I can now announce having at last reached the confines of this Queen City of our lovely and interesting valley, and that for to-day we have encamped just east of Lebanon county's capital. Whilst we propose to "take the city" also, it is not for any hearing not already gained nor for the righting of any wrong that I plead, except it be to arouse from its long, non-appreciative slumber this latter generation of noble Germans, to do greater honor and remember more kindly the bravery, industry, energy and heroic endurance, which its first American ancestors have here manifested.

Having come as far as Avon, where the soaking rains during this week suggested shelter in side-tracked box-cars or in the engine and tender that here a year ago,

(178)

long kept flying to and fro, like a weaver's shuttle, keeping the Annville and Myerstown street railway from crossing the P. & R. R. R. tracks, let us from this camp reach out to a few historic spots lying near by, and take time to reflect on the stream of earnest activity and travel that has surged about this place even as the angered Quittapahilla, having its rise near by, has this week lashed its swollen waves over cultivated fields and much-travelled highways.

Directly to the south of our halting place (Avon) lies the Stager homestead, which has a history of struggle and early peril worthy of note, and still contains an ancient landmark in the shape of an old house.

The following account will be of interest : In 1746 Frederick (?) Stager, (rather John Barnhard,) here took up 500 acres of land purchased from the proprietors for five pound sterling.   He reared a small log house upon it, presumably the same year or the one following, which is still standing.   It has marks of antiquity and interest to the curious in its outside stairway leading to the loft, its old-fashioned doors and quaint wrought-iron hinges, its fire place and its 14-inch wide oak planks for flooring.   One of his descendants, probably his son, Adam Stager, in 1782 reared the large stone farm-house that now constitutes the farm dwelling place.   It is large and commodious—a specimen and token of the growing wealth of these first families.   Among the old deeds still preserved among the family archives, is one of parchment, given by Michael Tice and Rudolph

Kelker, executors of said Adam Stager, conveying 200 acres of this farm to Frederick Stager. This deed was given June 5, 1818, and is recorded in our county courts, as is attested by this document in the handwriting of the ex-Gov. J. Andrew Shulze, who was then recorder

LEBANON VALLEY FARMER.

of the county. The original farm was thus divided and now is part of four farms, some of which—the western-most portion—is however still in the Stager name of the fifth or sixth generation.

The old homestead is the possession of Mr. Joseph Heilman, a descendant of the Heilmans of Heilman-dale. This gentleman holds a relic of gold that is truly worth more than its weight in that metal, inasmuch as he has refused a very handsome offer by some others of the family. It is a solid gold ring with a setting of some amber-colored, precious stone. This has been handed down from generation to generation from the first American ancestor of this family, Hans Adam (John Adam) Heilman, who received it as pay, in lieu of cash, from a neighbor in about 1738 or '39 for two months' labor, namely, grubbing away the scrub-oak and alder-bushes that grew as the first crop on what is now a part of the paradisaical valley of the Heilmans, northwest of Lebanon. This Hans Adam "was a man of stirring energy, and he not only made his arm felt in the clearing of the forest, but he took a prominent part in the religious and social affairs, and was one of the founders of the old Hill Church, and an elder of the same as early as 1745." The first house erected by him is still said to stand on the premises of his great-grandchild in Heilmandale. He married Maria Catharine Stager, and this shows the connection and how the Stager homestead is in part in Heilman hands. These early Heilman ancestors are buried at the Hill church. The Stagers, disinterred some twelve years ago from a private burial plot, now sleep at Kimmerling's graveyard. Mr. Joseph Heilman also found here recently an old copper penny bearing the image and superscription, not of Cæsar, but of another tyrant, viz. : King George the Third of England. The coin has on one side the face of this monarch with the name "Georgius III

Rex;'' on the obverse a harp and crown with the date
"1782.''

This old Stager homestead was the scene of a fierce
skirmish between the Indians and the white settlers
during the French and Indian war period, when one
white man was wounded and two Indians are said to
have been killed.

But being detained here for a while, let us look into
the malarious basin and checkered history of the once
busy but now idle and defunct Union Canal, leading by
our temporary encampment. This once enterprising
internal state water-way has an interesting history.
As long as the "great ditch" remains open, a relic of
the past, the present should be concerned to keep alive
the data of its construction and usage.

It seems that already in 1760, by authority of the
Provincial Assembly, a survey was made through this
valley to construct an internal water-way to connect
Philadelphia with Pittsburg, or the Delaware with the
Ohio. The route selected was up the Schuylkill to
Reading, and thence by the course of the Tulpehocken
and Swatara Creeks to Harris' Ferry, whence the West
Branch of the Susquehanna should afford a route
towards the western destination—a distance of 582 miles
from Philadelphia. The Revolutionary war put an end
to this movement. After the settlement of the struggle
for independence by the Colonies, other States moved
in the direction of canal building, and Pennsylvania
was likewise stirred from its slumber on this question,

when on September 29, 1791, the legislature took action incorporating a company to connect the Schuylkill with the Susquehanna by a canal. Such men as Robert Morris, the financier of the Revolution, David Rittenhouse, the astronomer, Dr. Wm. Smith, Provost of the University of Pennsylvania, and Tench Francis, were among its commissioners. Accordingly work was commenced on lands lying between Lebanon and Myerstown as early as the spring of 1794—just 100 years ago. Had my army of explorers been halted in their march a century ago, where I have made them pitch their tents to-day, they might have seen the first shovelfuls of earth thrown out of the ditch that still stretches throughout the length of our valley. They might also have seen such distinguished men as those named above make surveys in these parts. Let us therefore step softly, for any spot of earth pressed by the feet of such men as Rittenhouse, Morris or Dr. Smith, must be to the historian and student of any kind regarded as holy ground.

But alas! the enterprise failed, at least temporarily. After the expenditure of several hundred thousands of dollars operations were suspended in consequence of public remonstrances against the powerful corporation, until in 1811 this company, with another company known as the Chesapeake & Delaware Canal Company, reorganized into what became the *Union Canal Company*, which new organization pushed this old dream of internal State navigation into a reality. The State continued to grant aid by "a guarantee of interest and a monopoly of the lottery privilege." Hence by 1821 operations could be continued because of financial encouragement received. Six years later the project was completed, and in 1827 the first boat passed up this waterway, past Lebanon. This was the "Alpha of Tulpehocken." Not far from two millions of money had been expended in the construction of the canal—the first constructed canal in America. It is doubtless due to this "maritime highway" that the valley and county of Lebanon have attained to the wealth and commercial standing that characterize them to-day.

But another highway passes our temporary quarters here. It is the Berks and Dauphin turnpike, along which we have been slowly approaching this point, and which was constructed even before the canal was completed, viz. : in 1816 and 1817. It was also liberally aided by the State making large subscriptions to its stock. It is said to have cost an average of $3,800 per mile. Let us look into the faces of its travelers for the past seventy-five years. Before the day of railroads it was the one chief thoroughfare between Lebanon and Reading and between Lebanon and Harrisburg. It leads through the heart of the valley, and is known to have conducted in their travels such national characters as Presidents Van Buren in 1836, and William Henry Harrison in 1840, during their respective presidential campaigns—the former travelling east and the latter westward—going in opposite directions, as their politics

lay in opposite courses, yet both landing in the same
White House at last. There are men still living who
recall these campaign jaunts, and how a party of Whigs
accompanied Harrison from Myerstown in a tally-ho
coach, shouting themselves hoarse for old "Tippecanoe
and Tyler too." The same year that Harrison traveled
over this route his Democratic Vice-Presidential opponent (Col. Richard M. Johnson) also passed over this
highway. His admirers made the welkin ring all along
the route for this man, who, in the celebrated hand-to-
hand battle with Tecumseh, had the nerve to ride up
to the famous red-skinned chief and shoot him down
at his horse's head, though in the terrible scrimmage
about the dying chief he himself received severe
wounds.

But who shall call up the armies of great and small
men that have been carried over the Philadelphia &
Reading R. R. branch, stretching parallel with the pike
throughout the length of our valley, and sweeping by
our to-day's imaginary camping ground? What an
array of Presidents and would-be Presidents, of Gov-
ernors and legislators and politicians, great and small;
of learned doctors, and gifted ministers, and actors of
repute, and statesmen, and base ball clubs, and excursionists, and business men, and immigrants, and visitors
generally; what travelers for sight-seeing and for health
and for pleasure it has swept by this spot! Much of the
American world has gone over this line, and many a
foreigner, too—even the Liberty Bell preferred this

13

route home from the World's Fair last year—but no
one ever traveled through a finer country or a more
prosperous community for agricultural and honest
thrift. Hence, having reached the acme of reflection
and in thought capped the climax of this valley's past
prosperity, we will break up our camp and prepare to
march into Lebanon by another week or two.

CHAPTER XX.

THE HEBRON MORAVIAN CHURCH.

Just midway between our camping grounds of last week and the heart of the city of Lebanon, located on the pike, nestles the ancient village of Hebron. It was so named by the Moravian missionaries, who here founded a congregation as long as a hundred and fifty years ago; and the name was of course taken from Scripture, as this denomination, so full of the knowledge and spirit of Scripture, wove religious names and sentiments into their daily life in this new world, and especially the names of Bible localities into their settlements and congregational life. It is this very pretty custom of this church that has given us in eastern Pennsylvania such Bible-named communities as Bethlehem, Nazareth, Emaus, Hebron, Bethel and Lebanon, and such piously-dubbed settlements as *Gnadenhütten*, *Friedens*, and so forth.

The town of Hebron is older than Lebanon itself, and the first nucleus of houses here, together with its "*Gemeinlein*" (little congregation), of the United Brethren of the Moravians, is first of all spoken of in the early annals of this church as "on the Quitopehille." Here quite a colony of Germans had settled before 1742,

(187)

the year in which a hundred and twenty of the Moravians of the Bethlehem church, just founded, resolved, in their glowing zeal for the Master, to divide themselves into two halves, one portion of which should be sent forth as missionaries two by two, while the other half should abide and work for the former's support: Accordingly the province of Pennsylvania, and especially the frontier line, where mostly the Germans had settled, was selected as missionary ground. These disciples started on their evangelistic tours with a five weeks' circuit before them. The result of this enterprise was the establishment of their congregations at Lititz, Lancaster, Donegal, Bethel of Swatara, Hebron, "on the Quitopehille," Heidelberg, Tulpehocken, Oley, Emaus, Gnadenhütten, etc.—some of which have since become extinct, or else reverted to the Lutherans and Reformed, from among which denominations most of these early converts were made.

It would seem as if the names of the Apostles and other Bible characters had been given to these itinerant brethren, as we have them spoken of as Brothers John and Peter and Matthew and Joseph, etc., in the early annals of this church. It is quite likely, however, that they were simply known by their Christian names, inasmuch as "Brothers Joseph and John"—so frequently mentioned in the Diary of the Hebron church, the evident founders of this congregation—were doubtless the same as Brothers Joseph Powell and John Hagan, the missionaries, whose evangelistic tour led them to these parts. We find these same brethren a few years later active among the Indian mission at Shamokin (now Sunbury) founded in September, 1742, by the instrumentalities of such men as Count Zinzendorf, Bishop Boehler, Conrad Weiser (interpreter and leader), Henry Leinbach, and by John Martin Mack and wife, and Anna Nitschman.

The preaching of these missionary brethren, doubtless because of its pungency and its warm breath of Gospel life and because of a great lack of preaching by their own denominational pastors of these German Lutherans and Reformed, caused many of the most pious and earnest of them to fall in with this heroic movement for the dissemination of the Gospel. The thought of proselytism or denominational propagandism did not enter the minds of these unsuspecting men, thirsty for the water of life. Hence it comes that such leading Lutherans as Conrad Weiser and Peter Kucher, and such Reformed as Heinrich Xanders and others, became early identified with this church, many of whom remained loyal to the church of their adoption unto death, while some, as Conrad Weiser, returned to their first love, their mother church.

The history of the Hebron Church is a long and checkered one, full of interest to every student of history. We feel confident in saying that there is not a congregation within the county that has a more minutely written history than this one. The happy custom of the Moravian Church of requesting its resident

pastors to keep faithfully a full diary of events trans-
piring within the congregation, or occurring within the
community or country at large, has here preserved a
record of local and national events that is one of the

THE HEBRON MORAVIAN CHURCH.

richest treasures to the historian and antiquarian any-
where to be found throughout all this valley. The
writer was recently shown a pile of old journals—almost
as high as the publications that confronted Luther at
the Diet of Worms—which is simply a library of ten or
twelve large volumes of manuscript church records and
memorabilia of this Hebron *Gemeinlein* in the hand-

writing of its successive pastors. As this church, erected in 1750, and in part still standing on property now owned by Mr. David Fulmer (but alas! this portion of a once sacred structure, hallowed alike for its associations with church and state, is now used as a cow stable!) was used during the Revolutionary War as a place of incarceration for several hundred of Hessian prisoners, this diary is of intense interest during this period. The church was then in pastoral charge of Brother Bader, who is found, in the style of Cæsar in his Commentaries, to speak of his untoward experiences at this time. He commits to the safe keeping of his *Daily Journal*, a great many complaints and murmurings over the misbehavior of his rude prisoners and the none too exemplary conduct of their guards. Now it is their noise, then their carousals and sprees, that he complains of. Their filthy persons and habits form the occasion of still further criticisms. Again he has a tirade against the injustice of dumping the Lutheran Church prisoners upon him, when he was about getting rid of his supply.

But there are other things besides complaints in these journals. They speak familiarly of the trying events of the war as it progressed through its eight years of peril and hardship. It gives us the names of local leaders, such as Cols. Peter Grubb and J. P. De Haas, and others, and the accounts of their departure with their companies to the front of battle. It records the significant event of the surrender of Cornwallis, when that circumstance was first remarked abroad, and while, but as an unconfirmed rumor, it stirred all the land with intense excitement. To this important bit of news, this "Brother" later adds the significant postscript: "*War wahr!*"—"'Twas true!" As the present pastor of this church, Rev. E. S. Hagen, of Lebanon, has recently furnished a translation of these important annals to the Secretary of our State Historical Society, Mr. Jordan, of Harrisburg, we trust the public will some day be able to read all these interesting data of daily events in those trying times in their own vernacular. It would be a noble service to our community if the same were given for publication to some of our local public prints.

The writer was particularly interested in recently looking over this pile of ancient diaries, church-records, correspondence, and other ecclesiastical documents. One of these, an early, if not the original draft of the church building, gives the ground plan of this old edifice, which shows it to have been divided into a double house of a kitchen and two living rooms each, while the second story was the "Saal" or Prayer House, or "Oratorium," as it was styled in an inscription we understand to have been upon its wall.

Another record that was quite full of interest to us is the Communion Record, most carefully kept. The first volume contains those for the first 26 years of the congregation's independent life. It has the following introduction or preface, which I give in a free translation:

"Inasmuch as a small congregation has been organized by means of the efforts of the United Brethren, (independent since July, 1749), in the vicinity of Lebanon on the Quitopehille, in Lancaster county, and this congregation has been affiliated with that of Warwick until the close of 1749, and participated in the communions of that sister congregation, we resolved from the year 1750 to begin holding separate communions with this Lebanon congregation. Here it has been held since 1748, in the Lutheran church, (where in January a Brethren's Synod was held) until our own church should be completed, in which it has since been celebrated and continued according to the following *Conspectu* (Record)."

The first celebration, therefore, held here took place January 1st, 1750. The communicants numbered 23, and it was administered by Rev. Christian Rauch. The second communion was held March 1st, 1750, and was administered by Bishop Frederick Cammerhoff. The 9th communion was celebrated September 22, 1751, and in connection with Synod, according to this record.

This record mentions names, clerical and lay, in which we have become interested. The first pastors, beginning with 1750, were Christian Rauch, Christ. Herr, George Neitzer, Philip Mener, Richard Utley, Fred. Boehler and "Brother Bader."

There is an interesting narrative still preserved at Bethlehem, giving in the form of a diary a detailed account of the experiences of Bishop Cammerhoff in a visit he made to Shamokin in the winter of 1748. He

was accompanied by Brother Joseph Powell, and the
first day (January 6th) arrived at Macungie. Thus
by regular stages, and at the peril of their lives,
in the crossing of unbridged streams and trackless
snow-covered pathways, they made their journey on
horseback to and from their destination on the Susquehanna. The diary takes account of their stoppages at
Maxatawny, Ontelaunee, Heidelberg, Tulpehocken,
Hebron, etc. In Tulpehocken they called on George
Loesch and his family, who were among the Schoharie
settlers and later immigrants to Pennsylvania, who
united with the Moravians in 1747. The same journey
brought the Bishop and his companion also to the
houses of Peter Kucher and Heinrich Xander, two
leading members of the Hebron church. The communion record shows all of these to have been faithful
and consistent communicant members of the flock.
The Bishop in this journey took some provisions and
provender from these farmers to the Shamokin mission.

Concerning the personalities of these men, we learn
from the minute records of this church and other
sources that George Loesch was born near Worms in
1699. Immigrated with the Palatinates to America, and
settled in Schoharie, N. Y., in 1710; removed thence
to Tulpehocken in 1723, where he took up his residence just a mile northwest of Womelsdorf, already described, and where the land is still in the hands of his
descendants and some of the old buildings are still
standing. He became identified with the Moravian

Church in 1747, and remained in connection with the same until his death, which occurred in Nazareth, Pa., 1790.

Peter Kucher, or John Peter Kucher as he sometimes wrote his full name, was a native of Germany, and immigrated to America in 1732. He sailed in the ship "Loyal Judith," arriving in September of said year. He took up his residence just east of Lebanon. He was a Lutheran Christian and was connected with the Tulpehocken church, as appears from the list of 166 names of members, who in 1743 resolved to build a second church and declared to build up their congregation on true Lutheran principles. This declaration of principles and list of names is still preserved (given in Dr. Schantz's historical address recently published in pamphlet form) and contains among its signers the names of Peter Kucher and George Steitz, and others from these parts. The Moravian documents, however, show, in a carefully-kept register of its members, that he was converted to this faith in 1749, and communed with this *Gemeinlein* for the first time February 2, 1749. He was born according to this account in Waldau, Brandenburg, in the province of Saxony. His parents were George Peter and Barbara Kucher. He was in religion a Lutheran, in profession a blacksmith and farmer, received into the "brethren fellowship" during brothers John and Joseph's "land visitation," *i. e.*, missionary tour in Heidelberg, Feb. 2, 1749, was married Oct. 6, 1735, and had a family of ten children, whose names are given in order in this church record. In 1750 he

donated sufficient land for building and burial purposes,
so that in many respects he was a father to this Hebron
church.   The house which he built in 1761 (possibly
the second one) we found still standing.   It is a commodious two-and-a-half-story stone structure (a mansion
in those days) with wide middle hall-way and capacious,

THE PETER KUCHER HOMESTEAD.

easy central staircase of hard wood.   Although it has
not been occupied for some time and stands like a non-
animated corporal, great in its weird and forsaken soli-
tude, alongside the Quittapahilla and its old race-
course just two squares north of " Sweet Home," it yet
is a relic that is quite attractive to the student of his-

tory, in view of the knowledge of its once renowned owner, and the hospitable entertainment it furnished pastors and bishops and others. When it had life and soul this now hollow and ghost-harboring building must have been a home as fine as Mt. Vernon's mansion. What a hubbub there must have been in it, when the illustrious owner of that Southern mansion, as the General-in-chief of the Colonial army in revolt, sent a quota of 270 Hessian prisoners from Princeton and Trenton to the sacred house of prayer, where the occupants of this house statedly worshipped! The writer has recently visited this old relic when he accidentally discovered that it was the Kucher house. Seeing the sandstones in the second story front, the inscription upon which was illegible from a position on the ground, he clambered up an old rickety portico, from the roof of which he clearly read the following:

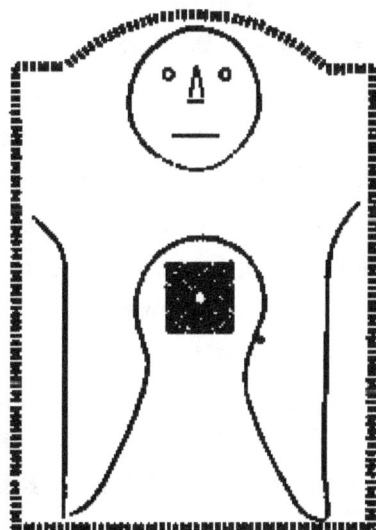

```
              17    ♡    61

            M . P E T E R

            K V C H E R .

            B A R B A R A

            K V C H E R I N
```

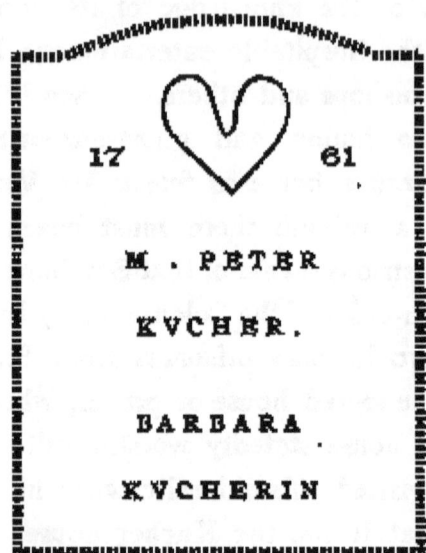

After my descent from this portico roof, I tried the
front-door latch and found it open, but nothing beyond
an echo and a weird, hollow strangeness greeted us from
within—not even the ghost of the energetic old pioneer
came to bid us welcome. We felt that if there was a relative of his still living, the same was committing an
unpardonable sin for letting such a valuable property go to ruins, and for allowing the walls of this historic homestead, resonant with the voices and foot-falls
of these pious ancestors, to fall into decay, when they
should be hung with the pictures and facts that tell its
story of piety and hospitality.

The record of Heinrich Xander is as follows : "Born
Nov. 16, 1702. From Rimlange, out of the Zurich
province in Switzerland. Religion : Reformed. His

trade, a smith and mill-wright (Müller-Bauer). Received into the church (Moravian) Whit-Monday, 1749, the 1¼ May, at a congregational day in Bethlehem. Took his first communion Oct. 1¼, 1749, in Warwick." This record was made in 1755, three years after the change from the old style to the new style of reckoning dates. Hence the fractional form in dates gives both reckonings—the numerator being the old style, the denominator the new style. Mr. Xander lived "five miles west of Kucher," according to Bishop Cammerhoff's diary. Here visiting bishops and brethren were generally entertained. His grave we found on the Moravian cemetery (Hutberg) near the old church in Hebron, south of the pike. The following inscription is found on his tombstone, lying flat upon the grave after the Moravian fashion:

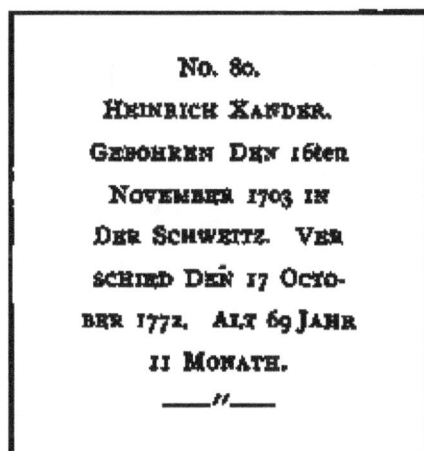

```
            No. 80.
        HEINRICH XANDER.
     GEBOHREN DEN 16ten
       NOVEMBER 1703 IN
     DER SCHWEITZ.  VER
     SCHIED DEN 17 OCTO-
     BER 1772.  ALT 69 JAHR
        11 MONATH.
          ——//——
```

The graves of other leading members of this flock,

many of whose birth dates back to the end of the seventeenth or beginning of the last century, are found here, but their names and other data are fast being obliterated from their memorial stones by the abrasions of time and weather. Yet we could discern the names of Johann Adam Kettering, born in Alsace, Germany, in 1698; George Hederich, born in Zweibrücken, 1706; Catharine Orth, born Kucher (daughter of Peter), born January 12, 1738; and the Buehlers, and Hains, and Bombergers, and Koehlers, and Graeffs, and Imhofs, and Schotts, and Uhlers, and others, who all sleep here their last sleep. But we must close this chapter. We trust it has stirred up a general desire soon to see much of the well-preserved local history kept here in print.

CHAPTER XXI.

Every one of my readers knows, or should know, that Lebanon was founded by Mr. George Steitz. He was a German, who before 1738 (according to a deed of that date mentioning his name and location here) settled here along the Quittapahilla on a tract of over 365 acres, covering the old part of the city, for which he received a patent from the Proprietaries of the province, dated May 22, 1753. Though there probably had been some town lots sold before Steitz laid out a part of his farm into building lots about the year 1750, this "laying out of the town" and sale of lots was the beginning of Lebanon. The enterprising German gave his town the beautiful Scripture name it now bears, possibly borrowed from or suggested by his Moravian brethren, whose Scriptural nomenclature stamped itself upon several of the townships of this county. It is more likely, however, that the township had been changed from Quittapahilla to Lebanon before the Moravians located here, and that the town's name was suggested by that of the township. Be that as it may, it is certain that, in spite of this naming, for a long time the village was known by the name of its founder, and that for

14   (201)

half a century after its beginning, the surrounding community did its shopping and frolicking and horse-racing and fighting in "Steitze-town."

We want to-day to take a walk around this old *burg* and see its outlying homes and other landmarks that guarded the old place before ever this century was born, or the village of Steitz had grown into the since enterprising maiden city of Lebanon. After this historic circumnavigation, we trust the walls, like those of Jericho, will fall, or the gates open, to let my army of explorers enter and behold the treasures of historic wealth buried within.

Having in my last letter led my readers to peep into the Peter Kucher house, who must have been Steitz's nearest eastern neighbor, we will go northward from here and surround the place by constant turns to our left. The old town-plots show John Light (Licht) to have owned the land north of Kucher, or east and north of the present city limits. We presume that the original deed of this property finds the name of Casper Wister, "the brass-button maker of Philadelphia," to have been the "party of the first part," inasmuch as it is known that he had first taken up from the Proprietaries the land immediately north of the Quittapahilla, the land that long separated Steitztown from North Lebanon, which latter village, at the opening of the Union Canal, rivaled its southern neighbor in business thrift and growth, and for some time bade fair to excel it in its strides towards a municipality. It seems not

yet to have forgiven its rival for stealing the march on
it, inasmuch as it prefers to remain "independent,"
though the growing "*Steitze*" has stretched itself in
well-graded streets, lined with homes, to its very doors.

Whether John Light had a house east of the city, or
whether there were two John Light homesteads on the
confines of this town, the writer cannot tell. He
knows of the old Light home, northwest of town, and
will presently lead his readers thither. But it would
seem that one family of Lights had resided east of our
city, as the old family burial-plot is found here, which
seems more distant than was common from the house,
if indeed the "Light Fort" was the first and only
Light homestead.* At all events, it is in the eastern
portion of the farm where the Lights buried their dead.
The family plot is found between Weidman and Lehman streets, east of Third, near to or part of what used
to be the old Fair Grounds. It is, however, stripped
of every vestige of fence or ornamentation. Only a
number of old gravestones, several of them broken,
mark the sepulture of this pious ancestry of our large
family of Lights. The question has come up to the
writer, whether these ancestors have deserved nothing
better at the hands of their present generation of prosperous descendants, than to be treated with the gross
neglect and forgetfulness apparent in these neglected

---

*The author has recently learned that there was another Light
homestead, east of Lebanon, last the property of Felix Light, a descendant, before it was replaced by the Penn'a Bolt and Nut Works

graves. Surely some simple mark of respect is due the
memory of these early pioneers, who paved the way to
the success and prosperity a later generation is reaping.
A little blooming shrubbery were more becoming than
a heap of rocks and debris ; an enclosure of paling more
fitting than a "commons" of stumps, and a few flowers
on Decoration Day more appropriate than a decoration
of cast-away tin cans and other rubbish by the desecrat-
ing neighbors. Oh! when will all men learn that
veneration and self-respect that shows itself in keeping
green the graves of the beloved dead, and step softly
over the mouldering bones of their ancestors? Oh!
when will Lebanon, as a municipality, gain authority
enough to prevent the theft and vandalism that discour-
ages such suggested improvements that would otherwise oft be prompted by grateful hearts ! *

Our visit discovered here half a dozen barely leg-
ibly inscribed tombstones. A few of them are broken
off and defaced. It is a wonder anything is left of them
after a century's exposure to time, weather and vandal-

---

*Scarcely had the above wish found a voice in this weekly corres-
pondence before one of many descendants of these Light ancestors, a
faithful and venerating scion, Mr. Asaph S. Light, editor of the *Lebanon Courier*, and the present postmaster of Lebanon, instituted
measures to have the mouldering bones of these ancestors taken up
from these uninviting surroundings and reverently reinterred in the
Ebenezer cemetery, about a mile to the northwest of town. Hence a
week after this chapter was originally written this old burial plot
was no more.

ism. The following are fac-similes of a few, in which
of the spelling and doubling letters and figures are peculiar, the latter indicated by a horizontal line over the
letter to be doubled. The first is of red sandstone,
others limestone or marble:

Hier Ruhet
Johannes Licht, ift ge-
bohren den 6 december
1720. Er ift ein Sohn des
Johannes und Maria
Licht, ist gestorben
6ten abril 1798. fein
alder war $\overline{7}$ Jahr
4 monat.

en in   ̈U. ̈ ̈ ̈ ̈ ̈ ̈ ̈ ̈
inder Ehe 48 Jahr
11 Monat. Gebohren
11 Kinder Wovon
noch 9 am leben 6 Söhne
3 Töchter. Gestorben
4 May 1798 Ihr
alter war 67 Jahr
6 Monat 3 Wochen
2 Tage.

Hier Ruhet im tod
IOHANNES LICHT
Er war gebohren im Iahr
1726 den 21ten Febr.   Lebte
mit seiner frav Anna inder
Eh.   48 Iahr 11 Monat.   Zevgte
11 Kinder Wovon noch 9
Leben 6 Sohn v. 3 tochter
Starb den 11ten Martz 1806
Ist alt worden 80 Iahr
2 woche & 3 Tage.

Liebe die Mich wird erwecken
Ars dem grah der sterhlichkeit
Liebe die mich wird bedecken
Mit der Kron der herlichkeit
Liebe dir ergeb ich mich
Dein zu bleiben ewiglich.

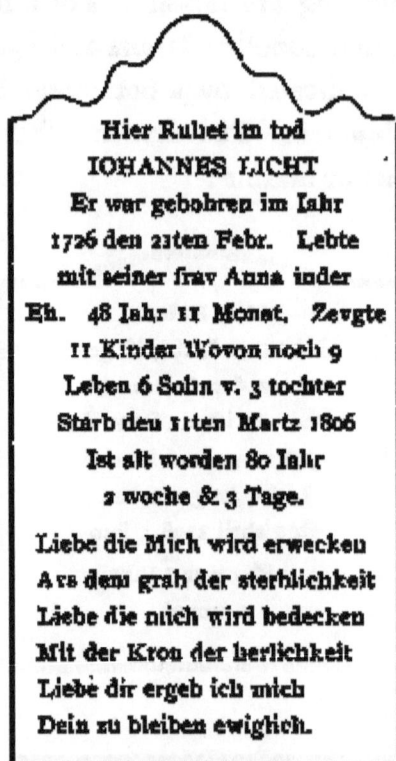

There is another stone, with an epitaph to the memory of still another *Johan Licht*, born 29th of December, 1767, died 10th of January, 1814. The relationship is very likely that of son to the *Johannes Licht* of stones No. 3 and No. 2, who, from the agreement in length of married life and the number of children, must have been man and wife. The one of stone No. 1 must have been a brother of same name or, possibly a cousin to the one of No. 3. Did one live east of town near this burial plot and the other northwest of town? The writer can not tell, only in the early history of

Steitztown the land east and north of the borough was marked as the farm of John Light. We know that one of these lived a little west of the corner of Tenth and Maple streets, where the old hip-roofed stone fort, constituting his abode, and erected in 1742, is still standing. We shall go to see it now.

THE JOHN LIGHT INDIAN FORT.

On our way to this landmark, however, let us take a peep into the old Lutheran parochial school-house, which formerly stood at the northeast corner of the Salem Lutheran cemetery, on Eighth street, until about fifty years ago. Its use having been displaced by the public school system, it was removed hither by a

Mr. John Harris, who turned it into a dwelling house.
It is a log building, now weather-boarded and slightly
changed. It is the present property of Mr. Charles
Swope, and is located on Canal street, alongside of the
stone quarry at the east end, and is at present unoccu-
pied. The rear door—double, like a shutter—is the
same that gave entrance and exit to the young Lutheran urchins of seventy-five years ago. It bears the
marks of their jack-knives to this very day. If it could
speak, what a story of woe and hardship it doubtless
could relate, as one generation after another of young
Germans were there graduated in their 𝔄 𝔅 𝔊's,
Psalters, Catechisms, and hickory birches.

But we repair to the Light Fort. Few of our citizens
may know or remember that there is such an historic
landmark so near. It is hid away from sight by other
buildings as you go out Tenth street. You want to turn
west on Maple at this point, and then it will soon appear
to view, just across the canal to the south. In 1738,
"the brass-button maker" sold to John Light several
hundred acres of land, who erected upon it, in 1742, the
stone dwelling and fortification here alluded to. It is
the best specimen near town of the style of roofing
adopted in those days for larger buildings. The custom
is Hollandish, and the style of roof generally termed the
Dutch hipped- or broken-roof. This is quite a massive
structure, and has a checkered history of refuge from
the savages, of the worship of God, of domestic toil and
struggle, and of liquor distilling.

The first owner, Mr. Light, was a Mennonite in religion, who opened his house for religious services, and it was so employed once a month for a long period. This community must have abounded with Mennonites in that early day, as quite a congregation is said to have assembled here. But the house was also built as a fortification against the Indian savages. It is provided with a deep, arched cellar, into which subterranean refuge a flight of stone steps still leads the way from the inside. Hither the neighbors were often compelled to repair, to find shelter from their enraged, insatiable foes. Sixty families took refuge in it at one time. Because of these retreats for safety, it received the name it has borne ever since, that of "Old Fort." We recently visited the building, but found the older part of the house rifled and deserted by all except a flock of English sparrows, a saucy-looking goat, and a family of colored folks, the last of whom occupy a few dreary-looking rooms. The writer has strong suspicions that during the best days of canal navigation this building was used as a warehouse.

The attacks made upon the whites by the Indians remind us of a record made in the Hebron Diary concerning a cruel murder of one of that flock, which occurred in Bethel, May, 1757. The mangled body was brought to Hebron for burial, and had we then stood where I have led my army of explorers in this chapter, in the north of town, we might have seen the funeral procession, a large throng, pass this place on their way to burial. The following record is preserved in the church annals of the Hebron Moravians : "May the 16th, 1757, John Spittler, Jr., was attacked and killed by murderous Indians, not far from his house at the Swatara. He was in the 38th year of his age, and settled the preceding year, in April, at the Swatara. His greatly mangled corpse was brought hither on the 17th of May, and accompanied by a large concourse of people, was buried here on our graveyard." Mr. Spittler was son-in-law to Mr. Jacob Meylin, whose relatives are still abounding in the county.

But we must hasten on and complete our circumference of the old town. Of course, we are only after the ancient, and are going in imagination "in ye olden time." Hence we have no trouble with cinder-banks and furnaces and canal-ditches and planing-mills and engirdling railroads; we can just take our walk across John Light's meadow and some grassy fields, past the fine old farm houses of Martin and Barbara Funck (who now sleep, side by side with his parents, in a private burial-plot near by, within an environment of cinder banks, stone quarries, smoking furnaces and puffing engines, he born Dec. 22, 1766, and died Feb. 17, 1838; she born Dec. 10, 1773, and died Jan. 15, 1853; while his parents' tombs show Martin Funck, Sr., to have been born Jan'y 30, 1732, and died Dec. 19, 1796, and his wife, Judith Funckin, to have been born Jan'y 19, 1732 and died March 4, 1812) still standing, the one erected in 1810, and the other in 1824. Soon after passing these landmarks we cross the Quittapahilla on the

west of town, to where George Gloninger's old home
has long kept its watch on this stream—which historic
homestead we shall visit at length in a later trip—and
from here wheel to the south and be ready to take a
glance at the spot where, before the middle of the last
century, was already found a church in common use by
the Lutherans and Reformed—known as the "Grubben
Church." This spot is about two miles south of the
town-center, on property owned by Mr. Jacob Brubaker.
But we have not time to abide here, where Revs. Conrad Templeman and J. Casper Stoever first dispensed
the Holy Gospel of the Son of God to their pioneer
flocks of German Reformed and Lutherans respectively.
We must bring our march to a close, and prepare by
another intermission of a week's rest and waiting to enter the city from the same direction the rebels invaded
our Keystone state in 1863 and 1864—from the south.
We prefer to enter the old town of Steitz from this direction, along the Cornwall pike—once a plank road—
because from this point of the compass and along this
celebrated and well-kept highway came the man who,
more than any other one man, changed Steitztown into
Lebanon—Mr. Robert H. Coleman. We will close this
chapter by quoting a poem that was written and read by
one of our most gifted and energetic citizens at a banquet, given some years since in honor of this second
builder of our city, who did more for Lebanon in pro-
moting its second growth than George Steitz ever did
in laying its foundations:

LEBANON: PAST AND PRESENT.

BY J. H. R.

There was a German gentleman whose name was Yorick Steltz,
He came across the ocean from a canton in the Schweitz ;
'Tis many years ago, you know, a hundred years and more,
Since this old German gentleman first landed on our shore.
He came with pluck and energy, with brains and money, too,
Just as the immigrants those times were always wont to do.
'Twas ere the foreign governments, to get rid of their scamps,
Dumped on our shores their anarchists, their nihilists and tramps.
For if they then had sent such scum across the raging main,
We'd hanged them higher than a kite or sent them back again.
He traveled inland from the sea, and when he reached this spot,
'Twas here that he resolved to stay, at which we wonder not,
For the valley stretched before him and the brooks went murm'-
    ring by,
'Twas charming to the senses, and most pleasing to the eye ;
And here he founded Lebanon, since grown to some renown,
But his neighbors, out of jealousy, called it old Steltz's town,
A name it bore for many years, two score of years or so,
Till Time, at length, with ruthless hand, laid Steltz's neighbors low.
And as it was to good George Steltz, so 'tis to us to-day,
A place not to remove from, but one in which to stay.
He builded better than he knew, for north, hid in the hills,
Lay coal to feed our furnace fires, our forges and our mills,
While southward rose an iron mount, awaiting, as we've seen,
The magic touch of master hand and sight of vision keen.
Between these mounts of coal and iron stretched valley, hill and
    wood,
A fertile land on which to raise the grain to give us food.
Here, too, were raised, as well you know, brave men of brawn and
    brain,
Who marched with Washington and Greene, with Lafayette and
    Wayne.

In eighteen twelve, and later still, in time of direst need,
They fought with Grant in Richmond's front, at Gettysburg with
    Meade.

But time moved on and changes came; the town it grew, of course,
And Peter Kahl's old stage gave way to Reading's iron horse.

We had our shops and factories and churches, schools and scholars,
Our stores were lit with gas at night, our bank-vaults filled with
    dollars.

So thus in peace we moved along, content to have it known,
That every decade showed our town had somewhat larger grown.

But suddenly there came a change, as if magician's hand
Had touched the town, and upward sprang new buildings tall and
    grand.

But I must not prolong this tale, and yet I fain would tell
How Colebrook furnaces came first, and then the C. & L.;

How then the business boom came on, and how we got our freights,
From north and south, from east and west, at low competing rates.

And then came forges, bolt works, mills, whose fires are burning
    bright,
Bank buildings and the new depot, and then the electric light.

And yet we'll name Mt. Gretna Park in Conewago's hills,
With pleasant paths and cooling shade, its lake and rippling rills.

And so where once a village stood when good George Steitz held
    sway,
A modern city upward rose and proudly stands to-day.

For this we've met in Banquet Hall—friends, you know all the rest,
How much is due to him who is to-night our Honored Guest.

CHAPTER XXII.

TABOR REFORMED CHURCH.

As we have decided to enter Steitz's town from the south, we will come in on the old plank road of the Colemans, whose last and illustrious scion, Robert H., has turned the sleepy village into a bustling city, and the rickety old highway of planks into a well-graded pike. This brings us into town on what is now Tenth street, and accordingly the first ancient landmark that meets our eye is the old Tabor church and school house. It is what is generally known as the First Reformed Church of our city—or, as a stone in its wall would indicate, the "Hoch Deutsche Reformirte Kirche." The present building was erected in 1792, and the school-house, it is believed, about thirty-six years previous to that date. From a succinct history of the church published two years ago by its present pastor, Dr. Klopp, we are enabled to cull many important data of its long, historic and beneficent life.

This declares the congregation to have been organized in 1760. The first deed, indentured June 10, 1760, whereby George Stites conveys to Frederick Steindorf, Felix Miller and Jacob Sollinger, "Deacons of the Dutch Presbyterian Church," and in trust for said

Church, the greater portion of the ground lying east
of the present church and constituting the old burial
ground, is still extant. It cost the original sum of five
shillings and the yearly rent of "one *Red Rose* in the
Month of June forever, if lawfully demanded." How
often this yearly rental has been paid since, the writer
can not tell. As the date has just passed (10th of June),
it is possible that the congregation feels it has dis-
charged its debt after having brought loads of roses
and other flowers to church in its annual Children's
Day Festival, celebrated last Sabbath—the anniversary
of this legal agreement. It might prove a worthy task,
but more difficult than last Sunday's service, to find
the grave of this generous promoter of "true religion
and piety" and deck it year by year with these choice
blossoms of June. This seems to be an unknown spot.
It is believed that he rests near his offspring and
relatives in Salem Lutheran graveyard. The writer
found the tomb of Mrs. Samuel Stites (Anna) in the
Womelsdorf graveyard, but knows not whether her
husband was a relative of George or not. This lady
was born March 3, 1817, and died March 28, 1846. A
similar requirement of the yearly rental of one red rose
binds also the Salem Lutheran Church of our city to
Mr. Steitz, and the Zion Lutheran Church, of Manheim, to the quaint Colonial founder and benefactor of
that town, Baron H. W. Stiegel. This last-named
flock celebrated last Sabbath the yearly Festival of
Roses, amid a jubilee of song and addresses, and in the

presence of relatives and lineal descendants from Germany, Virginia, New York, and Harrisburg. They are raising a fund to place memorial chimes in their spire in honor of this kindly and long enterprising, at last impoverished Baron.

Whatever generosity George Steitz may have manifested towards the early religious denominations of his day and town, it would seem as if the sheriff of the county a few years later seized his property, including this donated portion of his farm or town plot, consisting of lot numbered 136, and sold it, inasmuch as we find this same Reformed Church lot was sold by the sheriff and re-purchased by said congregation but three years after its very considerate sale by Steitz. At this time John Hay was sheriff of the county (Lancaster), and the purchasers of the tract, including these church lots, were Rev. John Casper Stoever, Christopher Wegman, Philip Greenawalt, Casper Schnebele, George Hock, Christian Gish, and John Ulrich Schnebele. These again sold in 1765 the church lots (upon which a log church had already been erected in 1762, situated on the northeast corner of the old graveyard,) to John Huber, John Rohrer, Jacob Smith, and Abraham Wideman, in trust for the "German Presbyterian Church." They paid five pounds in their second purchase to get back their improved property. This second transfer was made August 5, 1765.

Before the establishment of this church, the Reformed of this community worshiped for a generation at the Hill church, northwest of Lebanon, and at the "Grubben" or "Kruppen" church. The log house in which Rev. Conrad Templeman, the earliest pastor of these Reformed churches, lived, is still standing at Templeman's Hill, a mile east of Cornwall. It is in a dilapidated condition, and was found empty and forsaken by the writer in a recent visit thither. The associations of this energetic and faithful man of God, who spent the latter years of his life here in total blindness and suffering, while yet often ministering to his flock in holy things, should arouse an interest to keep this landmark from total decay.

According to an account of the event preserved by the Moravian pastor in the Hebron Diary, the first Reformed church was dedicated on the 18th of July, 1762. The name of Tabor was given it, evidently from the Mt. Tabor of Scripture. In this building the congregation worshiped regularly until June 12th, 1792, when the present stone edifice was erected. There was an interim of several years between the razing of the old church and the completion of the new, when the right of worship in their church edifice was kindly accorded this flock by the Salem Lutherans.

Improvements to the property have constantly been made since the beginning. In 1772 the church lots were enclosed by a dry stone wall, at a nominal expense of about $130, because of the very reasonable rates of labor and material at that day. On March 8, 1780, an adjoining property—the lot on which the present church

15

MT. TABOR REFORMED CHURCH AND CEMETERY, LEBANON, PA.

stands, and on which was then already standing the
stone house, now used as a sexton's house, but for many
years as a congregational or parochial school-house—

was bought of Philip Greenawalt and wife, for the sum of thirty pounds, or about $146. When this purchase was made, Gottfried Eichelbrener,-Michael Krebs and Rudolph Kelker were the trustees. In the deed transferring this property, the school is mentioned, which was built some twenty years previous to this date, and is still here as a witness to the value set upon instruction by our early German ancestors. A parsonage was purchased by a committee representing the different congregations constituting this pastorate at that day, viz., the Lebanon, Hill and Jonestown churches. They were Gottfried Eichelbrener, Nicholas Weiss, Jacob Lausher, Henry Dubs, John Tetweiler and John Bickel. This house stood many years on the site of the present handsome parsonage, corner of Chestnut and Spring streets. Formerly the services were all in German, and preaching but once in two weeks. Since 1828 English preaching has been regularly continued, though in constantly increasing proportions, until at present the German is limited to two Sabbath mornings a month.

The present building was erected in 1792-96. It was originally about 42x62 feet in dimensions. The cornerstone was laid June 26, 1792, under Rev. Ludwig Lupp's pastorate, when the Rev. William Hendel preached a sermon from Gen. xxviii. 12. The building committee consisted of Philip Greenawalt, John Gloninger, Anthony Kelker, Gottfried ,Eichelbrener, George Bowman, and Martin Imhoff.

An interesting Children's Service was held in connection with the laying of the corner-stone but a day or two previous, showing that such a thing as "Children's Day" in our churches is no new thing, and that Bishop Vincent, of the Methodist Church, can not boast being the founder of this now popular novelty. The fact is, all the good things in the Church of to-day are found in their prime and purity in the German Reformation churches, and were rocked into life by the Protestant Reformation of Luther, Melanchthon, Zwingli, Calvin, and others. From an old hymn or programme of exercises used on this occasion, over a hundred years ago, still extant, and a copy of which is in the hands of the Hon. Rudolph Kelker, of Harrisburg, whose grandfather was then Treasurer of this church, it would appear that they far excelled much of the modern *namby-pamby* stuff dished up with flowers and singing canaries on our "Children's Days."

The church was dedicated May 8th, 1796. We cannot account for the length of time consumed in building this structure, except, like the grinding of some sleepy mills situated along shallow and well-nigh dried up streams, the propelling power did not flow in faster. But the character of the structure does not suggest poverty. It is known to have cost about $6,500, and has upon it superior workmanship. There has been some extra expenditure to make it churchly in appearance. Over the windows of the west side, facing Tenth street, appropriate Scripture passages have been engraven. Beginning at the north they read as follows:

1st. "Lasset uns ihn lieben denn Er hat uns zuerst geliebet."—
I John 4: 19.

2d. "Der vernünftige Mensch lernet Gottes Wort gern, und wer
die Weisheit lieb hat horet gern."

3d. "Dieser Eckstein dieser Kirche ist gelegt worden, den 26ten
Juni 1792.

"Herr lass deine Augen offen sein ueber dieses Haus Tag und
Nacht. Hoere das Gebet deines Volkes."—II Chron. 6: 20-21.

4th. "Das Gesetz deines Mundes ist mir lieber denn viel Tausend
stück Gold und Silber."—Ps. 119: 72.

5th. "Thut Busse und glaubet an das Evangelium."—Mark 1: 15.

At its dedication Revs. Becker, Pauli and Hendel
officiated. But even still after a new church was secured, improvements were continued. In 1809 a pipe
organ was purchased, at a cost of $1,500. The present
wall surrounding the graveyard was built in 1816; the
steeple erected in 1827, and part of the cemetery, opposite the church, on Tenth street, bought in 1847, with
an additional part in 1848. The entire church was remodeled in 1844 at considerable expense, when the
vestibule end at the north was added. In 1845 the
church was incorporated, in which charter the following persons are named as Trustees, viz.: Jacob Arndt,
Leonhard Greenawalt, Christopher Reigert, Philip
Shaak, Sr., and John W. Gloninger; and the document is signed by Governor F. R. Shunk and by
Speakers William P. Wilcox of the Senate, and Find-
ley Patterson of the House. At the ratification meeting of the congregation, accepting this charter, held
May 24, 1845, a number of important resolutions were

adopted, relative to the spiritual care, the temporary support and the nurture of the youth of the church. The pew system was then adopted at English services, and other provisions pertaining to burial rights adopted. In 1857, John W. Gloninger and wife conveyed a lot of ground for burial purposes, situated west of town along the pike.

In 1860, sixty-eight members were dismissed to found St. John's Reformed Church of this city, of which the Rev. Dr. Henry Harbaugh, the celebrated author and Pennsylvania German poet, was first pastor.

In 1864, the Reformed Lebanon Classis, convened at Annville, divided and changed the pastorates in this community so as to constitute the Tabor Church in a separate pastoral charge. This necessitated the payment of $600.00 to the Hill Church for its interest in the parsonage, which was at once accomplished, the collections being over this amount, leaving the church treasury a handsome surplus of $206.76 from this effort. In 1869, the pastor's salary was fixed at $1,200.00 per annum. In 1872, the Lecture Room of the church was changed and Tabor Chapel built, which was enlarged and altered in 1890, thus adding an Infant Room and Pastor's Bible Class Room.

In 1877, at the establishment of St. Paul's Reformed Church of Bismarck, this church again lent a willing hand, and at its regular organization dismissed no less than eighty-six members from her fold. Another child coming out of the bosom of this mother church is the

St. Mark's Reformed Church, in the northern part of the city. It came to organized life in 1887, which again cost 166 of the living stones of the old church, and quite a number besides since that date. Templeman's Chapel, at Cornwall, cost the mother church another thirty of her members. Thus it is seen what a blessed "mother" this First or Tabor Church has been, and how she lives in her children, into whose youthful energies she poured of her best blood. Though venerable with hoary years and many deeds of beneficence, she is still bearing fruit in her old age, and strong enough to vie with any of her younger sisters or daughters in the work for God and humanity. She is well equipped with officers and working societies, and is one of the strongest churches in numbers and activities of this city. The handsome parsonage, which in 1890 took the place of the old historic manse on the corner of Spring and Chestnut streets, is a model of beauty and modern domestic convenience, and is alike a credit to the congregation and its pastor, under whom it was built, and a proof that this "mother" is not as yet going into decrepitude or decline. May she long live to bless mankind, and breathe among our younger churches and generations of citizens the earnest and godly spirit of her pious and sainted founders and earliest promoters!

The following pastors have served her:

After the pioneer services, preparatory to the founding of Reformed churches in this vicinity by Rev. Con-

rad Templeman, from 1727 to 1760, this local church
was served by

Rev. Frederick Miller, from 1762 to 1763.
Rev. William Stoy, from 1763 to 1768.
Rev. John Conrad Bucher, from 1768 to 1780.
Rev. John William Runkle, from 1780 to 1784.
Rev. Andrew Lorentz, supplied from 1785 to 1786.
Rev. Ludwig Lupp, from 1786 to 1798.
Rev. William Hiester, from 1800 to 1828.
Rev. Henry Kroh, from 1828 to 1835.
Rev. Henry Wagner, from 1835 to 1851.
Rev. F. W. Kremer, D. D., from 1851 to 1889.
Rev. D. E. Klopp, D. D., from 1889 to date.

From the Tabor *News* we learn that the following
persons constitute the present

CHURCH OFFICERS.

Pastor—Rev. D. Earnest Klopp, D. D.

Elders—B. F. Gingrich, William H. Boyer, William F. Spayd, William M. Snyder, J. Adam Becker, J. H. Witenmoyer.

Deacons—Frank Z. Miller, J. V. Smith, F. E. Bomberger, D. O. Mader, John A. Kleiser, Alvin H. Royer, Edward Brandt, George M. Snyder.

Trustees—Andrew J. Meredith, John H. Michael, Joseph L. Lemberger, Daniel P. Witmeyer, Jacob Brubaker.

Treasurer—William D. Rauch.

SUNDAY-SCHOOL, ORGANIZATION.

Superintendent—Joseph L. Lemberger.
Assistant Superintendents—Dr. E. P. Kremer, Miss Annie Matthes.
Secretary—Daniel G. Miller.
Assistant Secretary—John Shank.
Treasurer—Jacob B. Karch.
Librarian—Jacob B. Karch.

Assistant Librarians—Daniel M. Sharp, Frank Gleim, John Shank.
Teacher of Adult Bible Class—Dr. E. P. Kremer.
Organist—Walter Garrett.

Junior Department.

Superintendent—William F. Spayd.
Assistant Superintendents—William M. Snyder, Miss Savilla Witmeyer.
Secretaries or Librarians—Mrs. Jennie Shank, Mrs. D. G. Miller, Miss Millie Gleim.
Chorister—Mrs. D. G. Miller.
Organist—Miss Nora Light.

Infant Department.

Teachers—Miss Ella Ebur and Mrs C. G. Rauch.
Assistants—Miss Sallie Schram and Miss Gertie Reigel.

In the next chapter we shall stroll into the adjoining graveyards, and here come face to face with a large number of Lebanon's past worthies in the sacred and in secular callings.

CHAPTER XXIII.

FACE TO FACE WITH PAST WORTHIES.

BEFORE leaving the ancient shrine of Lebanon's first Reformed worshippers, let us spend an hour in company with the noble men and women who have been "gathered unto their fathers," and sleep their last long sleep in the shadow of the very church in which they worshiped and taught, or were taught, the way to heaven. The ancient burial ground that lies to the east of this historic church, contains the sacred ashes of not a few of Lebanon's most distinguished citizens of "ye olden time." In fact, this and Salem's Lutheran burial grounds contain almost all the dead of the first six or eight decades of this city's life. The Hebron Moravian cemetery contains a few, but its dead are mostly from the outlying country. The Reformed hold in sacred keeping a generous share of the ancient dead, and they keep their trust faithfully by looking well to the proper order of this last resting place of their dead.

June, the month of roses and robins—when every bush of the former glows with hundreds of bursting buds of beauty and fragrance, and every nest of the latter is ready to hold commencement-day and send

(226)

forth from its seminary of young bird-life its full-fledged
trio of red-breasted songsters—what a month of beauty
and bloom, of flowers and fragrance, of life and love!
Just the month in which to visit a graveyard! The
chirp of the sparrow, the sweet song of the robin and
the thrush, and the exciting chatter of a score of swallows, which, as evening approaches, take their winged
chariot races through the air—each racer urging on his
feathery steed with noisy ado—combine their notes and
noises to overcome the otherwise painful silence of a
lonely burial ground. And so the waving grasses, and
the blooming and budding life on every shrub, help to
mellow the otherwise too sombre consciousness of being
in the presence of decay and death. Moreover, these
natural evidences of life and beauty serve as a token
and type of the land of reunion with the sainted dead,
where are found perpetual bloom and eternal life.

It was on a perfect day of this maiden month of summer that the writer, pushing away the tall grasses,
wended his way from grave to grave of the past
worthies that sleep in this Reformed "city of the
dead," and with reverent heart and by the aid of well-
worn epitaph, communed with the generations that
have passed. Here he found the graves of Pastor Lupp
and his wife, during whose energetic ministry the present stone church edifice was erected in 1792–6. He
learned elsewhere that this man of God was a native
of Germany, and that for a while after coming to
this country he taught school, and conducted devo-

tional services in private houses, before assuming the duties of the ministry. He had served a charge in and surrounding Manheim, and was instrumental in founding the first Reformed church at Harrisburg, before removing to Lebanon, where he busily pursued the labors of his holy office, in season and out of season, for a period of about twelve years. That he was generally beloved is evidenced from the fact that the Lutheran pastor, Rev. Mr. Kurtz, assisted the Rev. William Hendel, of the Reformed Church, in the funeral services, by preaching a second sermon, and by the witness of the Moravian Hebron Diary, whose pastor records various instances of fraternal intercourse with him. Describing one of Rev. Lupp's confirmation and communion services, which said pastor attended by invitation, he adds: "There was at these solemn services, which continued six hours, a general loud weeping in the church, and the young hearts were quite carried away." He was doubtless the author of the responsive service which the children of this parish rendered on the dedication day of the church, to which allusion has already been made, and which is a model for propriety and churchliness. It is a service in which the leader, the children and the choir respectively take part, and the program is entitled: "Zum Knæbchen Fest." Pastor Lupp was buried here in this delightful month of June, almost a century ago, according to the following humble marker that still distinguishes his grave:

Hier ruhet ein grauer Haupt

LUDWIG LUPP,

12 Jahr Prediger in Libanon
Gebohren den 7 Januar, 1733
Gestorben den 28 Juni, 1798
Alt 65 Jahr, 5 Mon. 21 Tagen.

Es war mein Beruf und Amt in deiser Welt
Zu lehren was meinem Gott und Jesu wohlge-
fällt.
Zu predigen das Evengelium rein und treu
Den Sündern rufen zur Bus und Reu;
Nun adieu! Fruende, folget meiner Lehr und
Wort
So werden wir einander wieder sehn in jener
Himmelspfort!

Not far away sleeps his wife and companion, with a similar sandstone marker.

We find here the grave also of even an earlier pastor, and one who must have been beloved by his flock with extraordinary affection. It is the Rev. Johann Conrad Bucher, serving this flock an equally long period of a dozen years, beginning with 1768. He was a noted man in his day for his service both in the Church and State. Born in Switzerland, his father, intending him for the ministry, gave him a thorough academic education at the Universities of St. Gall, Basle, and Gœttingen, where he gathered into an autograph album, still extant, the autographs of his celebrated teachers, Wagelin, Zollikoffer, J. L. Mosheim, the great church historian, and others. At the age of twenty-five he came to America. He was soon enlisted into the conflict that was being waged between the English Colonies and the combined forces of French and Indians. Parliament, after the defeat of Braddock and the subsequent year of disaster, passed an "act providing for the appointment of German, Swiss and Dutch Protestants as officers," in order to enlist the greater sympathy of these classes of immigrants to the English cause. Accordingly, Bucher was appointed as Second Lieutenant in the First Battalion, Pennsylvania Regiment, and after the fall of Fort Du Quesne, he rose to First Lieutenant, April 19, 1760, and was stationed at Fort Louther (Carlisle) to defend the frontier against Indian raids. He participated in Bouquet's expedition in 1763 for the relief of Fort Pitt, which had been assailed in Pontiac's Conspiracy, in which march the famous battle of Bushy Run was fought. Mr. Bucher was gradually promoted for his brave services, until he rose to a Captaincy in Colonel John Penn's Regiment.

In 1765 he again participated in an expedition against the incursive Ohio Indians under General Bouquet, when the celebrated capture was made of the captive white men, women and children these enemies had in former years carried off; among whom was the noted Regina Hartman, who sleeps in one of the "God's acres" of our valley. While on their return from this expedition, and while encamped at Fort Bedford, an association was formed by the officers of these Pennsyl-

vania Regiments to ask the Proprietaries to make a
new purchase of land from the Indians and grant to
each of them a reasonably large and commodious tract
as a plantation. Their efforts succeeded, and thus there
was ceded to Captain Bucher, in 1769, no less than 616
acres in the Buffalo Valley (Union county), and 570
acres in the Bald Eagle Valley (Center county). February 26, 1760, Lieutenant Bucher married Mary Magdelena, daughter of George Hoak, of York, and three
sons survived him to perpetuate his name and fame in
Dauphin and Huntingdon counties. During 1765-68
he resided at Carlisle and began the service of the Reformed Church as minister, officiating in churches at
Falling Spring, Hagerstown, Sharpsborough, Fred-
erickstown, Middletown, Hummelstown, Quittapahilla,
and Lebanon, as well as Carlisle. In 1768 he accepted
a call from Lebanon, and removed hither in the spring
of 1769, his field extending over large parts of what are
now Lebanon and Lancaster counties. Such exposures
and trying services, however, tell on any constitution.
The strain was too much for the soldier-priest, Bucher,
and he succumbed to heart-disease on the 15th of
August, 1780, while officiating at a marriage ceremony
in the family of one Killinger, on the Quittapahilla,
near Millerstown (now Annville). So esteemed was he
that, though a hearse was awaiting to carry his body
back to Lebanon, his friends would not consent to it,
but carried the dead pastor on their shoulders to his
home—a distance of five miles. He lies buried among

the honored and loving flock he shepherded so faithfully. A sandstone marks his tomb, with the following inscription :

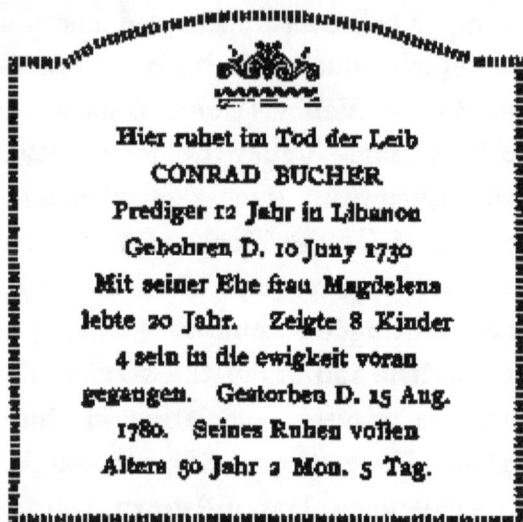

Hier ruhet im Tod der Leib
CONRAD BUCHER
Prediger 12 Jahr in Libanon
Gebohren D. 10 Juny 1730
Mit seiner Ehe frau Magdelena
lebte 20 Jahr. Zeigte 8 Kinder
4 sein in die ewigkeit voran
gegangen. Gestorben D. 15 Aug.
1780. Seines Ruhen vollen
Altern 50 Jahr 2 Mon. 5 Tag.

One might here find enough material for somber reverie and meditation. The grave of a learned scholar, a brave and honored soldier and a beloved pastor! Yet here he sleeps in a bed as humble as the lowliest. Truly

"The boast of heraldry, the pomp of power,
And all that beauty, all that wealth, e'er gave,
Await alike the inevitable hour ;
The paths of glory lead but to the grave."

Two other pastors of this flock lie buried on these Reformed graveyards, old and new. In the old, near the church, is the tomb of Rev. William Hiester. A large flat stone marks his resting place, which is inscribed as follows :

Zum Andenken
des
EHRW. WILHELM HIESTER
Prediger 28 Jahr in
Libanon und den umliegen-
den Reformirten Gemeinden.
Gebohren den
11 November 1770
Zeugte 11 Kinder 7 Sohne
und 4 Tochter.
Starb den 8ten Feby 1828
Alt 57 Jahr 2 Monath
und 28 Tage.

[Here follows a long rhythmic appeal
to the flock to be faithful and meet their
pastor on high.]

The Hebron Diary has many complimentary things
to say of him also. Rev. William Hendel preached his
funeral sermon, February 11, from the text, Deut.
xxi. 16.

In the new cemetery, opposite the church, on Tenth
street, a beautiful monument marks the resting place of
the congregation's pastor who gave it the longest unin-
terrupted term of service (a little over 38 years) of any
of her many shepherds, viz., Rev. Dr. F. W. Kremer.
From all accounts he was an ideal pastor, much beloved by his people. He had but one other charge besides—that of Grindstone Hill, near Chambersburg, Pa.

16

"While conducting the funeral cortege of Mrs. Samuel Heilman to the Hill church, he was suddenly translated to his reward in heaven, on the morning of June 14, 1889, his horse and carriage being struck by a fast express on the Lebanon Valley R. R. at a crossing near the Hill church. . . His name and life have found lasting place in the hearts of those who so long enjoyed his faithful ministry." The following epitaph tells the brief story of his services and death:

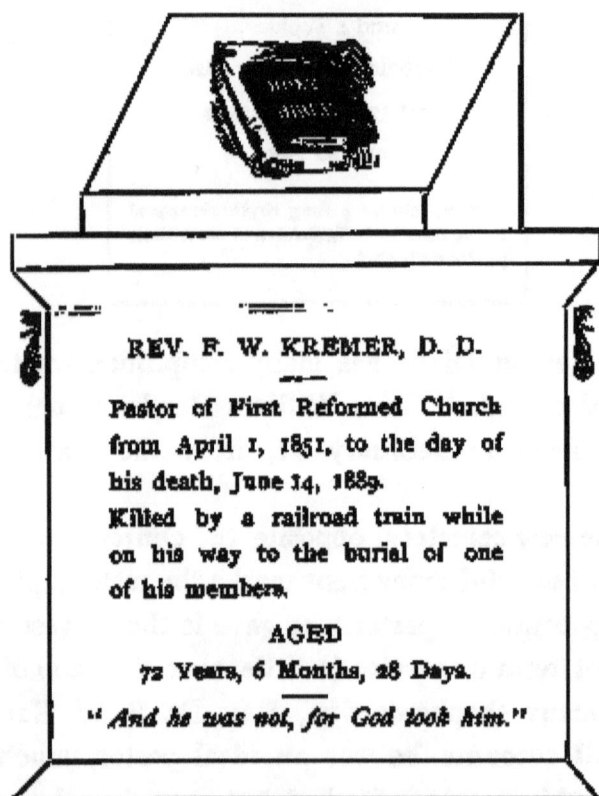

REV. F. W. KREMER, D. D.

Pastor of First Reformed Church from April 1, 1851, to the day of his death, June 14, 1889.
Killed by a railroad train while on his way to the burial of one of his members.

AGED

72 Years, 6 Months, 28 Days.

"*And he was not, for God took him.*"

Besides these pastors, these ancient graveyards contain the sacred ashes also of Mrs. Rev. Stoy, Mrs. Rev. Hiester, Mrs. Rev. H. Wagner and Mrs. Rev. Kremer. Rev. Philip Gloninger, a Reformed minister, also sleeps here amid the large family of kin, but we shall have occasion to refer to this rather illustrious old family in another chapter, and therefore omit further allusion here. Other notable graves are those of the Eckerts, Marks, Heisters, Hubers, Pfeiffers, Dr. John B. Mish's, Karchs, Moores, Elliotts, a long row of Greenawalt graves, in some of which sleep Revolutionary sires; the Kelkers, including that of Anthony, treasurer of the church when the present edifice was erected; and the Gottfried Eichelberner of that day, and Esq. |Peter Lineaweaver and wife, and many others. We think we found also the long-lost grave of George Steitz, the founder of this city and donor of this church lot. Now we would not be guilty of putting the bones of even such an old worthy as Steitz into another man's grave. We read in Scripture that such an hasty and promiscuous burial once took place, where the body of a certain dead man came in contact with the bones of the buried Prophet Elisha, and it had the effect of stirring the newly-extinct body into life and new animation. We neither care to produce a sensation nor to call back any one that has passed from life, but we have strong suspicions that by some amateur "Old Mortality" the tomb of George Steitz has been made to read George Stein. I will offer my argument, and let the curious either prove or disprove the same. In the center of this old burial ground, east of the church, is an old-fashioned tombstone, north of a fenced-in lot, on which is found a considerable amount of artistic ornamentation. It shows the marks of the sculptor's chisel since originally placed—evidently to retrace a part of the inscription that was becoming indistinct. It left half of this epitaph intact, because still legible, but found the stone so hardened and coarse-grained as to make it impossible to engrave the fine text of the other half that was fading, and so the vanishing phraseology was capitalized. Thus what now reads "Zum Andenken des George STEIN" was certainly at first "Stein" if not "Steitz" with the "tz" so faded that this employed artist of a few decades ago *guessed* the surname of one more common. This is the theory. The partial alteration, with the other half untouched, becomes at once evident to any one visiting the spot. The dates of birth and death seem to be "1717" and "1787" respectively, but are almost faded. We invite the curious to examine the case for themselves, and let every "Stein" of this community or elsewhere, having here buried an old ancestor, now speak, or the coming Steitz monument might be by mistake here erected over the remains of the wrong man.

There is but one more grave that we shall visit, and then take a reluctant leave from a charming spot and an interesting old companionship. This is the grave of Mr. Curtis Grubb. By his side sleeps his son, who died when a youth of seventeen, and two large flat stones, lying side by side, mark their resting places. Mr. Grubb was a brother of Captain Peter Grubb, who figured prominently in Revolutionary times. He had charge of the Cornwall Furnace, which was then casting cannon for the Colonial armies. Curtis was equally enthusiastic for liberty, and exerted himself for its promotion at home, while his brother gave his energies to the cause in the field. Thus we find him creating sentiment among his neighbors, serving on various committees, and taking a leading part in this community for liberty. It is said that he, with his family, were regular attendants of this church, though living in the Cornwall Hills. The following epitaph records his life and demise:

In Memory of
CURTIS GRUBB, ESQR.,
of Cornwall Furnace.
Who departed this Life
the Twenty-second Day of
January, One Thousand
Seven Hundred and Eighty-
nine.
Aged Fifty-eight Years.

———

Stop Wanderer,
Come, learn how vain this life below,
How swift thy days pass by,
More swift than any stream they flow
On to Eternity.

CHAPTER XXIV.

A HALT ON MARKET SQUARE.

WE turn away to-day from the lovely and ancient "*God's-acres*" of the Reformed, where peacefully sleep so many of Lebanon's past worthies, and from the church they built and in which several generations have worshiped, where we have spent our time in the past two outings, to visit the similarly historic house of God and old graveyard of the Lutherans at the corner of Eighth and Willow streets. But this walk leads us across the Central or Market Square of our city, and so we must make a halt here before going on, and mingle, in this chapter, with the living rather than the dead. For here there is no resemblance to the place we last visited and the one we are next bound for. This is a scene of stirring life, and few that move about this center of our city every day do ever think that they are only a few blocks from the cemetery—that the distance from busy life to tranquil death is so short, that from noon to evening is but a brief span, that Central Square lies so near Cemetery block. But we will not look too gloomily upon this stirring scene, and will therefore shake off for to-day the grave-clothes from our spirits. We are between two cemeteries; but we are now in neither. We

are in Lebanon's Market Square. Only it is a square
without the market—"Hamlet" with Hamlet left out.

> "Es wær ken leichte Sach zu mir
> Wans Marik-House muesst dort weck,
> Mei Herzt hængt dra, as wie 'n Klett
> Es macht mich krank, ich muss ins Bett!
> Ich schlupp mich in 'n Eck!
> O *move* sell Marik-Haus nimmermehr
> Eweck fon sellem *Center-Schquare!*
>
> * * * * *
>
> "Sel Schquare war g'macht for'n Marik-Haus nei,
> Der *William Penn* hot's g'sad,
> Er hot die Insching g'frogd dafor—
> Sie hens gegrant *forevermore,*
> Un 'a muss ah nau dort sei :
> Was wær's dan for 'n Marik-Haus *Schquare,*
> Wan's net for sel alt Marik-Haus wær?"

But, alas! Even William Penn, George Steitz, and
H. L. Fisher, the York poet, combined, could not keep
the old "*Marik Haus*" in the Lebanon Square. It
had to go with the other relics of the olden time before
the march of improvement which was ushered in when
the second growth came to Lebanon, about a dozen
years ago. But most of my readers will recollect the
old market sheds. Some of the oldest of them will remember the Fourth of July morning when old Dr.
Lineaweaver's gig graced the roof, though the Doctor
had carefully locked his shed the preceding night to
prevent the patriotism of the young Americans of that
day from manifesting itself in such and other similar

demonstrations. And while it stood, on either side of
Cumberland street, what fine specimens of Lebanon
county produce, in men and maidens, in cheese and
cabbages, in radishes and red-beets, in sausages and
sauer-kraut, it presented once or twice a week! Since
men live on country produce and settle into aggrega-

CENTRAL SQUARE, LEBANON, PA.

tions of towns and cities, market places have been a
necessity and they have always given the world true
phases of life.

But we are not here with provision basket in hand
to make purchases. We have come with the chron-
icler's pencil to take a few notes of the historic land-

marks, in the shape of old homes that still surround this market-square of Steitz's town-plan. Coming from the south, we begin with the first old house that faces it on the west corner, and find it a pre-Revolutionary

MARKET SQUARE, LEBANON, PA.

(Looking South.)

Showing Filbert's Store, The Mish House, and "American House" in the distance at off-set.

relic. It is now a public hostelry and known as the American House.   Its fine stone front elevation still bears two stones which tell much of the story of its erection. The inscriptions of religious sentiment, following a custom of certain German provinces, here read as follows:

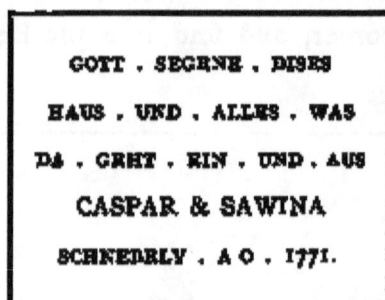

GOTT . SEGRNE . DISES

HAUS . UND . ALLES . WAS

DA . GEHT . EIN . UND . AUS

CASPAR & SAWINA

SCHNEDRLY . A O . 1771.

MAURER   IN LEBANON

HEINRICH REWALT

1771

As far as we know the house has a good name. We can speak from personal experience that it sets a good table, but we have a strong suspicion that some other spirit than the one invoked in this date-stone has sometimes "blessed" some who "here go in and out," since the private residence has been changed into a public house, with license for the sale of "fire-water." It is now the property of Mrs. Kleiser, and the stopping-place of the country mail coaches. In 1855 it was the property of Dr. John W. Gloninger, who added a third story to it.

From here, past a few business houses, whose histories are a checkered story of transfers, we come to the stuccoed and yellow-painted stone house of Mr. John W. Mish. This is another old property, the main part of it having been built, as near as can be remembered, and as a stone in the wall, but under the plaster, says, in 1762. It is the old Krause house, built, it is believed, by John Krause, the great-grandfather of Mrs. Mish, who was a daughter of a younger John Krause, who was the son of David Krause, who was the son of John, Sr., who was married to a daughter of Adam Orth (Regina), whose wife in turn was a daughter of Peter Kucher. All the connections here are prominent, the Kuchers, Orths, Krauses on Mrs. Mish's side, and the Mishes and Weidmans and Bickels, of the county, mixing their blood in Mr. Mish's veins. Their family of children promises fairly to carry the name and honor of a worthy ancestry into the time and generations coming, into whatever clime or country they may chance to wander. The house is large and commodious. It has served various purposes. In the beginning of this century it was a hotel or restaurant. There is still an old inside shutter swinging in the northern room which records the bill of 12 segars against ex-President James Buchanan as due Andrew Huber, and having been purchased on a Sunday, September 15. We know this noted character, when an aspiring young lawyer, used to practice at Lebanon county courts. During Mr. David Krause's occupancy, and at the first establishment of the county, the main front room of this house was used by him as Prothonotary's office. This Mr. Krause was born in this township in 1750, and was a farmer by occupation. In the back yard of this old mansion there used to be a large Swiss barn, where were stored the products of a portion of the original Peter Kucher's large farm, into the possession of which he came by the marriage of Regina Orth, the granddaughter of this celebrated Moravian leader. Part of the same farm is still in possession of the family, and improved by the lovely country residence of Mr. Mish, just a mile south of the town center, and at present occupied by their son Robert. The Revolutionary war spirit fired the blood of young Krause, and, leaving his farm in other hands, he associated himself with those striking for the cause of freedom from a foreign yoke, and became conspicuous as a commanding officer of a local company, and as Commissary in Colonel Greenawalt's Battalion.

Among the many family relics still kept here is Commissary Krause's Book of Accounts, in which are found his receipts and expenditures as a Governmental officer. Among other entries, the writer was interested to find the following :

"August, 27, 1777. Cash paid to Coln. Adam Orth, for 3 corts of wood, to be delivered to the Hessian prisoners, at 12 sh. a cort."

There is found here also Mr. Krause's Docket as Justice of the Peace, which is most carefully kept. It shows that on one occasion he imposed the fine of 7 shillings and 2 pence upon a certain man for swearing. We have thought if every similar offense were now followed by the same penalty, Lebanon would soon have a revenue that would be able to bring us the best street paving, a sufficient number of electric lights, and an adequate supply of the best water.

After the Revolutionary War, Mr. Krause served in the State Assembly from this county (then Dauphin) before and after the adoption of the State Constitution, in 1790. For two years he served this county also as a Commissioner. After the establishment of the county of Lebanon, Governor Snyder appointed him one of the Associate Judges of the county, which position he held at the time of his death, in 1822. His sons, born here, added honor to the name—the youngest, David, gaining a very fair reputation as Private Secretary of Governor Shulze, Deputy Attorney General of his county, associate editor with General Simon Cameron of the *Pennsylvania Intelligencer*, editor of *State Journal*, and as Judge of the Montgomery and Bucks Judicial District, while John, father of Mrs. Mish, served as Attorney General of Pennsylvania. The present head of this old homestead, Mr. Mish, is well known for his business ability, having served in important positions and filling now the office of Secretary and Treasurer of the Lebanon Gas Company.

Next we come to the corner building, at present (1894) undergoing extensive improvements, in being changed in form and purposes from an ordinary corner store-stand into the imposing wholesale liquor house of Mr. Filbert. This house also is historic. It is the celebrated Philip Greenawalt's old home, or rather the site is the same; for when Colonel Greenawalt lived here the building was a double-story frame hostelry, which was later changed into a store and occupied by Mr. Frantz, from whose hands it passed into Jefferson Sherk's and thence into Mr. Diller's and now into Mr. Filbert's. But as we are walking in the olden time, we see none of these later changes and only note the brave and doughty old Colonel as he goes in and out here, loaded down with honors and a multiplicity of years. A native of Germany, he came to America in 1749 and located first in what is now Lancaster county, but later came to this side of the South Mountain ridge. At the outbreak of the Revolution, he was commissioned Colonel of the first battalion of Lancaster county. He was associated with Washington in the New Jersey campaign of 1776 at Trenton and Princeton, and at the Brandywine he received the commendation of his commander-in-chief for efficiency of service. He was appointed by his state as one of the commissioners to take subscriptions for the continental loan, December 16, 1777, and during the war's darkest period he did noble service in collecting food, forage and clothing for the suffering soldiers at Valley Forge, for most of which he is said never to have been recompensed. His regiment was composed of local companies, commanded by such then well-known captains as (1) Casper Stoever, (2) William Paine, (3) Philip Weiser, (4) George Null, (5) Michael Holderbaum, (6) Leonard Immel, (7) Valentine Shoufler, (8) Henry Schaeffer, (9) Daniel Oldenbruck. These names often occur in local history. Colonel Greenawalt died in this place, in 1802, at the good old age of 77 years, highly honored and respected by his fellow citizens. He sleeps in the old Reformed cemetery, and around him have been gathered many of the scions of his large family.

But we must go on. Crossing Cumberland street, we come to the Gloninger homestead—for several generations past the property of this distinguished medical family. Although none but Gloningers have gone in and out of this fine old habitation as occupants for the century that is past, still the building was not erected by any of them, but according to deeds in hand—and the family hold a chest full of these parchment documents, and many precious heirlooms besides—was built by Gen. J. Philip DeHaas. The original sale of this corner town-lot, by Steitz, was made to this historic character shortly after the town was laid out, and the character of the house to be erected upon it was specified in the deed. So it is from this corner that this Revolutionary warrior went forth, and to this identical house that he came back as his home. Arriving in this country with his father, from Holland, in the year 1739, as a mere child, they settled near this place. He had already given conspicuous service to his adopted country in the French and Indian war. He shared in the officers' land-grants along the West Branch of the Susquehanna at the close of this period, upon which lands in Clinton and Center counties his descendants settled and are still abounding. For ten years—1765-1775—he was one of the King's justices of the peace, residing in this house. There are some very interesting resolutions extant, which were adopted at a meeting of the citizens of Lebanon after the arbitrary measures of the Crown, closing the port in Boston, as early in the Revolutionary agitation as June, 1774, which resolutions bear his name as chairman, and which meeting was held in the house of Captain Greenawalt. The following are the resolutions as copied from Dr. Egle's history:

"At a meeting of the inhabitants of Lebanon and the adjoining townships on Saturday, 25th of June, 1774, holden at the house of Capt. Greenawalt, whereof Major John Philip DeHaas was chairman, to take into serious consideration the state of public affairs, it was unanimously declared and resolved:

1. That the late act of the British parliament, by which the port of Boston is shut up, is an act oppressive to the people of that city and subversive of the rights of the inhabitants of America.

2. That while we profess to be loyal subjects of Great Britain, we shall not submit to unjust and iniquitous laws, as we are not slaves, but freemen.

3. That we are in favor of a Congress of Deputies, who shall act in behalf of the people for obtaining a redress of grievances.

4. That we will unite with the inhabitants of other portions of our Country in such measures as will preserve to us our rights and our Liberties.

5. That our countrymen of the city of Boston have our sincerest sympathy, that their cause is the common cause of America.

6. That Messrs. Philip Greenawalt, Thomas Clark, Michael Ley, Killian Long and Curtis Grubb be a committee to collect contributions for our suffering brethren.

JOHN LIGHT, *Secretary*."

J. P. DeHAAS, *Chairman*.

This document shows what spirit of patriotism heaved the bosoms of these gallant citizens, most of them of German ancestry, against whom the false charge has sometimes been made that they were indifferent to the cause of freedom, or totally lacking in patriotism. The Revolution formally opening, we find DeHaas, speedily chosen colonel by Congress to command the First Pennsylvania Battalion. He set the gunsmiths of Lebanon to work to make the muskets for his regiment. His battalion merged into the Second Penn'a Batallion, after his Canada campaign in 1776, which he henceforth commanded, until he was promoted to a brigadier-generalship, in which capacity he served until 1779. That year he removed to Philadelphia, where he died in June, 1786, "leaving his property here to his wife, Elenor, and son, John Philip, as the executors of his estate." And thus this house came to be purchased by the Gloningers, who have held it ever since.

But reserving for another chapter the history of this

17

family, when we reach the original homestead of the first Gloninger immigrant on the banks of the Quittapahilla, we will pass on to the next homestead, commonly known as the "Weidman House," but now owned and occupied by Dr. Joseph L. Lemberger and family.

This house is a model of preservation, and well shows the character of the old kind of masonry. The date of erection is not quite certain; some claim it to have been built by the DeHaas heirs, and that it is more than a century old. It was long occupied by Edward Godwin, Esq., a native of England, and for a long period a leading legal light of this town. He was the associate of such prominent attorneys of our state as James Buchanan, Jenkins, Montgomery, etc., of Lancaster, and the Elders, Fosters, Auricks, etc., of Dauphin counties, who often must have stepped across the threshold of this historic house. Then it became the residence of Mr. J. Andreas Shultze, and was occupied by him when elected to the gubernatorial office of our state. From Governor Shultze it passed into the hands of "Gen. John Weidman, and because of which fact it is often called the Weidman house." From Weidman it came into possession of Mr. Joseph L. Lemberger, whose family now occupies the mansion, with one room re-served for the prosecution of the well-known Central Square drug business. The house is still good enough to shelter another governor, but whether it shall occur, will depend on the present occupant or his successors. We have no objections to have it take place now.

CHAPTER XXV.

OUR walk about the old Market Square of Lebanon was interrupted just as we came to the fine stone mansion of Mr. Lemberger's, whence stepped out, in 1823, Andreas Shultze, to fill the Gubernatorial chair of our State, after having held a number of other official positions of the county and the State. It would be pleasant to dwell a little while in company with this cultured and popular Governor of our State, whose election to a second term of this high office, in 1826, was unprecedented in point of majority, he receiving not much less than 75,000 votes, while his opponent, John Sergeant, received but about 1,000 votes. But we must hasten on, so as to complete our walk about this old town square, which is lined with historic landmarks, leaving the relatives of the Governor in the enjoyment of the honor reflected upon them by this illustrious kin.

Before leaving, however, the residence whose historic walls are still lighted up by the brilliant fame of this once renowned owner and occupant, we must recall, with a certain degree of patriotic and race pride, at this season of Independence Day reminders of Revolutionary sires and leaders, that when that illustrious French patriot and ally of our American colonists struggling for freedom—General Lafayette—revisited our country in 1824-25, it was this same Governor Shultze who officially welcomed him to Pennsylvania State soil amid great pomp and civic display, at Morrisville, on the west bank of the Delaware, opposite Trenton, N. J. It should stir our present citizens with local pride at this Fourth of July season, that in a parsonage of this valley was born the child (the great-grandson of the most distinguished German pioneer of this State—Conrad Weiser), who in this valley grew to manhood, here for a time preached the Gospel of Jesus Christ, then followed here a mercantile business, afterwards holding offices of public trust and honor, and later marched out of this identical stone mansion to fill the highest office in the gift of our Commonwealth, and as such had the honor to ride in that brilliant pageant of State officials, of mounted field and staff officers, of bands of music, of processions of artillery and infantry, of Revolutionary heroes, of artisans and farmers, of gaily dressed riflemen, in which he – the son of our valley and the distinguished citizen of our own Lebanon town—was the State's representative and spokesman. Riding in a barouche drawn by four brown horses, he followed next the distinguished visitor—Lafayette—who, with the famous Judge Richard Peters, of the Revolution, the friend of Washington, was drawn by six cream-colored horses, with outriders in livery, mounted on horses of the same color—and was followed by another

barouche similar to his, containing Governor William-
son, of New Jersey—on that proud day in September
(28), 1824, more than seventy years ago, when this
magnificent pageant came from Trenton and entered
our City of Brotherly Love by the Delaware.

But we are far from home and must hasten back, and

CENTRAL OR MARKET SQUARE, LEBANON, PA.
(Looking North.)
Showing the Gloninger Residence, the "Weidman House," etc.

must complete our historic pilgrimage about Lebanon's
old square, even if attended by less of pageantry and
honor than was so largely shared by one of its quondam
residents. The house next north of this "Gubernatorial Mausion" is the present property of Grant Weid-

man, Esq., who purchased it from William Stoever, of
West Myerstown—a lineal descendant of Rev. Johann
Casper Stoever—who, as executor of his father Jacob's
estate, made the transfer about twenty-five or thirty
years ago. Jacob Stoever here carried on the printing
business, and from this place shone forth over the territory of the county, at least once a week, for about thirty
years, the first and long the only newspaper enlightener
of the place — *Der Libanon Morgen-Stern.* Jacob
Stoever was a son of Frederick Stoever, the squire, and
he was the youngest son of pastor J. Casper Stoever.
Who had possession of this property before Stoever, we
could not learn; but the place suffers not by comparison
with others in reckoning up the good influences that
have gone out thence. The Stoevers and Weidmans
both being Lutherans, the early members of these
families all sleep in Salem Lutheran burial ground.

The property next north to this, situated on the S.
W. corner of 9th and Spring alley, and now occupied
by offices and as the residence of Mr. J. K. Funck, was
first sold by George Steitz to Anastasius Uhler, March
4th, 1759. There are documents showing that it was
again conveyed by said Uhler to Daniel Strow, who conveyed it to Andrew Beistle, at whose death and according to the terms of his last will, Messrs. Christopher
Wegman and Jacob Souders, as executors, sold and
transferred the property August 17, 1782, to Henry
Shaffner. The lot then had a frontage of sixty-four feet
on Market Square. The northern half of same, with

house, was conveyed, at Mr. Shaffner's demise, by Jacob Goodhart and Daniel Stitchter, executors, to Mr. Adam Grittinger, June 16, 1837, which same property was bequeathed by Mr. Grittinger to his son, Henry C., the present owner. The Shaffners we know to have been inter-married with the Greenawalts and otherwise highly reputed, while the Grittingers, father and son, served in various honorable positions, as well as the present occupant, to give this place a history.

Opposite Spring alley, on the site of the building now occupied on the first floor by the Post Office, where cluster other interesting facts of history, let us especially imagine the former frame building out of which came to play or go to school in the early decades of this century the boy Alexander Ramsey, whither his mother, whose maiden name was Kelker, on becoming a widow removed with her family from Hummelstown. Mr. Ramsey as man rose from one station of honor to another, until he became in 1849 first Territorial Governor of Minnesota, holding office four years, and making important Indian treaties, and for the United States Government negotiating large purchases of their lands. Mayor of St. Paul in 1855, and elected Governor of the State in 1860-63, he was the latter year elected United States Senator from Minnesota and served twelve years, and in 1879 became Secretary of War, and in 1882 a member of the Utah Commission.

Were we to continue our walk on Ninth street to the north we should find much more buried history to exhume, but we shall simply lead our excursionists about the old Market square, and so must here step across Ninth street to the east side and complete our walk. The building that here at present forms the northern offset of this square is the second structure of the Zion Evangelical Lutheran church, which just has completed the semi-centennial of its life, an event worthy of note. The first building erected here in 1844 was a stone edifice and rough cast in plaster. The lot before this date was the property of Jacob Shaffner, then residing at Marietta, and the purchase of it was made by Jacob Stoever, one of the trustees, for the newly organized congregation coming out of the mother church (Salem) and led by the pastor, Rev. Jonathan Ruthrauff, on the score of language, church discipline and revival measures. The spot has an interesting history, because of its fifty years of eloquent preaching of the gospel by such men as Rev. Ruthrauff, Drs. Wedekind, Gotwald, Schindler, Rhodes, Reinmund and Dunbar ; by the long and successful efforts here made in the salvation of souls; by the men it sent into the ministry ; and by a long list of conventions held of every description, missionary, Sunday-school, conference, synodical and General Synodic, of which we have not time to speak at length.

We come next, on the south, to a property now occupied by three stores (tea, jewelry, and shoe) presenting a frontage of about 66 feet, and mentioned in the original town-plot as Lot No. 65. The property is owned by Mr. Frank S. Becker, and has been in the family since 1810, when his grandfather, Jacob Goodhart, the clock-maker—whose name rivals that of Jacob Gorgas, in the number of times it appears on the face of the old-time, high corner-clocks—purchased the ground with the improvement of a log house, weather-boarded, for the sum of 426 pounds, "lawful money of Pennsylvania," from John and Catharine Fasnacht, who were the executors of their father's (Conrad) estate. This Conrad Fasnacht was a butcher, and evidently · here carried on his business of selling, if not of slaughtering. Deeds are at hand to show that this property was part of the original town-plot, purchased at sheriff's sale as property of Nicholas Henicke, by Peter Kucher, August 5, 1764, who sold and conveyed it, April 1, 1774, to Adam Orth and Catharine, his wife, (Kucher's daughter) who in turn conveyed same to John Keller, October 22, 1785 (whose wife was a daughter of Adam Orth), who again sold it, May 4, 1792, to said Conrad Fasnacht. Probably the most noted occupant of the old homestead that first occupied this central spot, of whose residence here we are certain, is the long-lived clock-maker, Mr. Goodhart. On the establishment of Lebanon county, we find him representing this district for several years (1815-16) in the State Legislature. Upon the acceptable creation of the borough of Lebanon, in 1821, he was elected as the first Chief Burgess, which office he held for two years. He also served as County Treasurer from 1826-29; was universally recognized as a reliable surveyor, conveyancer and scrivener; and was for more than thirty years a Justice of the Peace, many times elected by the people and twice appointed by the Governor for usual terms of several years each. We find his name also among the first trustees of the Lebanon Academy, established in 1826. But whatever good may have been done by Mr. Goodhart in all these official positions, we think that his "grandfather-clocks" will do more to perpetuate the fame of his honest thrift and skill, in the hundreds of homes they are to-day brightening, measuring off by musical ticks the minutes, and by clearly ringing strokes the hours of the day, than by any other great deeds this long familiar German worthy of Market Square performed.

The next house—a relic of the last century—is the property of our nonagenarian friend Mr. Simeon Guilford. It was part of the John Keller estate when the above-mentioned transfers of the next adjoining lot were made. It is very likely that in this same house—still standing and occupied by Mr. Guilford, Sr.—lived Mr. Keller, the saddler, at the beginning of this century, and we can imagine his children—playing here with their cousins, among whom was the future illustrious statesmen of Indiana—a native of Lebanon—Godlove S. Orth, who died but twelve years ago, after having held many of the most important offices in the gift of his country and adopted state. Mr. Guilford, the present aged occupant, is a native of Northampton, Mass., and came to town at the opening of the Union Canal in 1823—an energetic, youthful civil engineer of twenty-two. The same State improvement or institution brought to town also another once honored citizen, Mr. William Lehman, who lived a year in Gov. Shultze's house after the latter was made Governor, and later at the Canal (Ninth and Maple). These, together with the president of the Canal Company (Mr. Mifflin), have been kindly remembered for their noble deeds to this town in the work of opening up this internal waterway, by having streets in the northern end of our city named after them. Mr. Guilford has occupied this home since 1830, here reared a noble family, and from it has gone out to a long continued career of usefulness in the erection and operation of Swatara (Schuylkill county), and Dudley (long known as Donaghmore) furnaces. He married, May, 1830, Miss Catharine E. Doll, and their oldest son with his family living in the adjoining house, a citizen and physician of high repute, keeps the declining days of an unusually long and prosperous journey from becoming dreary and dark. In the same house, or a stone house preceding this, had lived before him for some time Anthony Kelker, a revolutionary lieutenant, and a most worthy citizen. To this same stone house of Guilford's was brought the Hon. William Henry Harrison, when as a candidate for the United States Presidency he made his visit to Eastern Pennsylvania. Simeon Guilford, who was an ardent Whig and enthusiastic advocate of

"The old Tippecanoe, Harrison and Tyler, too,"

and one of the local Committee of Entertainment, went all the way to Reading to meet this honorable ex-soldier, and accompanied the party in a tally-ho to Lebanon. Although stopping at what now is the Central Hotel, then the Buck Hotel, he took the distinguished citizen and coming President to his own home for a few hours' social intercourse. All this is history worth remembering as clinging to the solid masonry of this old landmark. [P. S.—Mr. Guilford died in Feb'y, 1895.]

The corner property where now stands the Lebanon National Bank, is the same where formerly stood a stone building, in which dwelt, in 1830, Mr. William Moore, who was instrumental in establishing the first bank in Lebanon, and became its first president. The lots of the town plot covering Mr. Guilford's and Mr. Moore's residences are numbered 66 and 67 respectively. Mr. Moore was a highly honored and leading citizen, filling various offices in the gift of his townspeople. He lies buried in the Old Reformed graveyard, and his grave is marked by a suitable stone. This corner of Ninth and Cumberland was long occupied by a mercantile house, where, I think, Oves & Moore carried on the dry goods business for years. The bank building displaced it about ten or twelve years ago, when it removed hither from where the dining room of Eagle Hotel is now located.

The site of the Eagle Hotel, on the opposite corner, has quite an illustrious history. Here Frederick Stoever, Esq., the youngest son of the Rev. John Casper Stoever, some time in the latter half of the last century, erected a store building and carried on business, and for some time the office of "a 'squire." Later Peter Lineaweaver, the third American by that name, came into possession of it and changed the store into an old-time hostelry, where stopped more of the old-time visitors and transient guests than possibly at any other house in Lebanon. In its halls it was a frequent thing to hear the voices of the most brilliant legal lights of East Pennsylvania and the political visitors of that day. The house has since been rebuilt, and its reputation for high grade service is known far and wide. We are hindered for lack of space to enter into any further history of the house, or the families that have resided here, or even to give the past occurrences of the old Henry DeHuff manufactory of copper and silver-ware that used to occupy the space south of Eagle Hotel, thus completing the Square. The readers can find Mr. Stoever's grave on Salem Lutheran burial-ground, and the Lineaweavers on the Old Reformed. The latter's family was intermarried with the Tobys, the Klines, and the Krauses, all of whom are well known in Lebanon and its vicinity.

We trust our halt on this Square has convinced my readers that this heart of Lebanon has coursed with good blood and sent out to bless the world and fight its battles a greater array of strong and manly men than any similar spot of earth, of equal dimensions, in any city of our land.

CHAPTER XXVI.

Our halt on Lebanon's Market Square has detained us longer than we had at first contemplated. Thus having mingled with scenes of stirring business life in the past two chapters, let us without much ceremony bow ourselves out of these surroundings and transfer ourselves to the corner of Eight and Willow streets, where we will find a monument of old-time church-love and a volume of ancient local history in the landmark of the Salem Lutheran church edifice that shall now occupy our attention.

This church, as well as the Old Reformed—the only two congregations of Lebanon that have an age corresponding to or antedating that of the town itself—has its second local habitation. Before Mr. Steitz had laid out this town, and an aggregation of dwellers here had made the beginnings of a village, what few Lutheran residents were found in this immediate territory worshiped with their brethren of the surrounding country, either at the Hill church, about 2½ miles to the northwest, or else at Krupp's (or Grubben) church, about 2½ miles to the southeast, but mostly with the latter. Here really Salem Lutheran church was born, probably

as early as 1735, and led through its infantile life.
Rev. J. Casper Stoever was both founder and pastor of

SALEM LUTHERAN CHURCH, LEBANON, PA.

the Lutheran side, and Rev. Conrad Templeman of the
Reformed—for it was a union church. While there are

still to be found traces of the foundations of this church edifice and a graveyard to mark the spot, unfortunately there are no records at hand to tell us aught of its history. The Hebron Diary makes mention of a Moravian Synod having been held in the Lutheran church, while *their* church (completed in 1750) was being built; and as there was no town church this allusion must evidently refer to this church, or else to some temporary house of worship in the village of Hebron or the cluster of houses that then served as a nucleus for the future Lebanon. Mr. Steitz himself having been a Lutheran may have made early provision for church services in the town he founded. Be that as it may, with the growth of Steitz's-town developed also the necessity and desire for a Lutheran church. And thus we early find the Grubben church weakened by the loss of the membership of the town church, into which it gradually merged—Rev. Stoever being the pastor of both. Remnant official records of this pastor and a few relics, such as chalice and flagon for communion service, bearing dates "1757" and "1760," are the only relics extant of these early Lutheran church beginnings here. Among these entries are the marriages of Francis Reynolds to Catharine Steitz, Feb. 25, 1731; George Reynolds to Eleanor Steitz, Dec. 12, 1738; and John Peter Kucher to Anna Barbara Koppenheffer, Oct. 6, 1735.

The first documentary evidence, however, of a separate Lutheran organization in the town limits that is in hand, is the deed conveying the present corner lot on

Eighth and Willow streets to Jacob Bickel, Daniel Stroh, Philip Fernsler and Michael Reiter, trustees, for the use of the Lutheran congregation, and this is dated March 13, 1765. For this piece of ground "the yearly rent of one red rose in June, in every year forever hereafter, if the same shall be lawfully demanded," was to be paid. The same year a school-house was erected on this lot, which was used for worship until the first church was built, three years later. At this time a most earnest, even solemn circular of appeal for financial help was sent out to other Christians, carefully certified as to its genuineness and authority, by Pastor Stoever and several civil officers, empowering the Brethren Frederick Yensel and Christian Fremdling to receive such contributions. In this document allusion is made to the fact that hitherto "divine and religious services" had been held with great inconvenience in private houses. From the help thus received, the congregation was enabled the following year, 1769, to erect its first house of worship in Lebanon. It stood on the southwest corner of the present graveyard, facing Willow street. It was a log structure which served well its purpose for thirty years, until the present massive church edifice displaced its use in 1798. Among the relics of this first building are still found the timbers in what is now "Oswego House" on Cumberland street; an iron rooster which graced the old steeple, now in the possession of Mr. Geo. H. Reinoehl, and several pewter communion services are kept at the parsonage. The

18

writer had the pleasure of seeing these recently, together with an altar-cloth of fine linen, bearing an early date (1773), and found the tankards beautifully engraved thus:

The bread or hostien-plate bears the monogram "I. CH." which, we presume, stands for "Iesus Christus." The bell, also used on this building, still swings in the present steeple.

While the earliest records of even this church are lost, there is at hand a Church Book of records begun by the pastor, Rev. F. A. Con. Muhlenberg, in 1773. From this date entries of official acts are faithfully made and historical data are well preserved. This protocol preserves the facts of importance concerning the building of the present edifice. According to it, the corner-stone was laid June 8th, 1796, when Rev. Emmanuel Shultze, of Tulpehocken, preached in the forenoon, Rev. Hendel, of the Reformed church, Tulpehocken, in the afternoon, and the Rev. Schlegel (probably Moravian) in the evening. The names of the church officers then were as follows:

Pastor—Rev. George Lochman, A. M.

Trustees—Michael Rieder, Philip Fernsler, Jacob Stieb, and Samuel Meily.

Elders—Conrad Reinoehl and John Schnee.

Deacons—Peter Shindel, Frederick Embich, and George Schott.

Most of these names are still represented in the present membership of the church. We have in hand an illustrated "Life of Washington" in German (a translation), printed here in 1810—but a decade after the President's death—which bears the imprint of John Schnee as publisher. Quite an enterprising literary venture for a little town of Pennsylvania Germans! But then Lebanon had patriotic giants in those days, some surviving soldiers, who had fought with Washington the battles of the Revolution.

The second edifice of this church, now lacking but a few years of completing its first century of service, is substantially the same, externally, as when first built.

There have been added about fifty years ago (1848), two vestibule corners to complete, with the originally appended massive stone steeple, the quadrangular shape of the structure, while its interior has been wholly remodelled. It experienced another general renovation in 1866. Originally it had the very common style of church arrangement in olden times, namely, a high ceiling with steep, bulky galleries, the organ at one end and a high goblet-shaped pulpit with sounding board at the other. In the midst stood the altar with banistered enclosure. An exact model of this original church, the workmanship of Mr. H. W. Embich, janitor, on North Eighth street, can now be seen in the latter's home. We had the pleasure of seeing here some other old relics of this original building, and learning some data of importance in the special services held in the past century in this ancient temple of divine worship. The same church servant has also kindly given us a look into the towering belfry of this massive edifice, from which one or the other of two silvery-toned voices has for a century been calling its worshippers to service, or else announcing the death of its members, or else proclaiming to the city the outbreak of some accidental conflagration, or the birth of some national holiday.

These bells have a history. The oldest and smallest one, weighing about 1,000 pounds, was used in the first building, and was cast in London, England, and shipped simultaneously with a similar one for Trinity church, Lancaster, Pa. It bears an inscription as follows : "For the Lutheran Congregation in Lebanontown, Lancaster Co., in the Province of Pennsylvania. Pack & Chapman, of London, Fecit, 1770." The larger bell was cast by Jones & Hitchcock, Troy, N. Y., in 1854, and weighs over a ton. In a storage place in this lofty belfry we were shown also a few antique locks, made for and long used at the doors of the church. They are immense copper and iron constructions, about

8x10 inches in dimensions, and were made, according to the inscription on exposed plates, by "John Rohrer, Locksmith, Lebanon, 1798," and "Jacob Smith, Locksmith, Lebanon, 1798," respectively. Besides the latch they are provided with five bolts or rails, enough to lock out such foes as heresy, schism, the world, the flesh and the devil. We here found also a curious looking basket, not much unlike the one of bulrushes in which the infant Moses was rescued, but having found quite a different use. We were told that when in 1847 or '48 the steeple was painted, this contrivance was used in connection with tackle and pulley to prevent the necessity of building a scaffolding, and that in this invention Messrs. Nagle and (John) Dreher completed their contract of painting unharmed.

To come back again to the story of the first bell, it was less than a decade before this English product was hung in its place in the first church, when it began, like the old Liberty Bell of Philadelphia to "proclaim liberty throughout the land and to all the inhabitants thereof." Its sound must not have been very musical to the several hundred Hessian prisoners, who were quartered here for some time after their capture at the battle of Trenton, N. J., but it was about this kind of *irony* these hateful English allies deserved.

The pastors who have served this congregation since its foundation are here mentioned. We would like to give brief sketches of all, but have space only to give names and dates. The record is as follows:

It would be interesting to enter into an account of the arduous labors of these servants of God at this place, but that would require volumes, and is not the present purpose of these letters. Suffice it to say that as far as we know all have given diligent service for the upbuilding of this parish, and that the combined labors of all, together with the coöperation of the congregation, have resulted in building up one of the strongest and most influential churches of Lebanon.

Only one of these pastors is buried here, viz.: Dr. W. G. Ernst, who died in 1849. A small marble monument near the rear entrance of the church marks his resting place. Upon it are epitaphs to the memory of his mother (Elizabeth Ernst, wife of Rev. John Frederick Ernst, born March 22, 1747, died January 31, 1826) and other relatives. His own reads thus :

In Memory of
Rev. WILLIAM G. ERNST, D. D.,
who was born in Sussex Co., N. J.
October 30, 1786.
He preached the Gospel for
34 years, 29 of which he was
Pastor of this Congregation.

Through the merits of his Savior he
entered into his eternal rest
Sept. 1, A. D. 1849.
AGED
62 yrs. 10 months.

"Blessed are the dead which die in
the Lord from henceforth: Yea, saith
the Spirit, that they may rest from
their labors: and their works do follow them."

The third pastor, Rev. Kurtz, a younger brother, we
think, of the Rev. John Nicholas Kurtz, of Tulpehocken, also lies buried in the county, but at Jonestown, being then also a part of this parish.

The list of pastors numbers some of this denomination's most noted and scholarly ministers. Rev.
Muhlenberg was a son of the distinguished patriarch,
and it is altogether probable that as his father was still
living during this son's pastorship here, he visited
him and thus most likely preached for him; so that
although without a record stating the fact, we be-
lieve that the illustrious Henry Melchoir Muhlenberg
preached also in this city, and that in Salem's pulpit.

From this mother church have gone out Zion's in 1844 (from which has branched Seventh Street Lutheran,) and Trinity in 1885. Though vast the influence it exerted for so long a period, the church to-day is abreast in numbers, influence and activity with the most active of the city, and does not have any signs of age, save in the influence it wields and the merited respect it receives from the younger churches of the city.

A step out of the rear door of this ancient structure and we are in the original cemetery, where are sleeping the first few generations of worshipers here. What a book this is to read! Familiar names that were once on every lip, have here been chiseled on cold marble with the significant "In Memoriam!" The truth is, despite the somberness, a cemetery has certain indescribable charms for most of us. It is the place for deep thought, for silent revery, for next to real communion with our departed friends.

This graveyard has the old enclosure of a stone wall to keep out the vagrant, the irreverent, the vandal and the busy world that surges by, with neither time nor inclination to check its rushing gait for a thing so utterly foreign and chilling to its arduous zest as that of a burial place. It is a pity that this wall has too often shut out also the presence, the sight and the tender care of the surviving friends of these departed ones; for there is not apparent here the tender care, which the worth of the departed, the name of this church, and the conspicuity of this street corner deserve. Could not steps be taken to beautify this spot like Mt. Lebanon, and a fund be raised to keep it in repair? We should

ANOTHER VIEW OF SALEM LUTHERAN CHURCH, LEBANON, PA.

be glad to give a transcript of many old tombstone inscriptions found here, but we have space for but a few.

Some of the oldest have so faded that they are no longer legible. It is believed that such an one marks the grave of Mr. George Steitz ; for upon the most reliable tradition of his descendants, despite any former supposition to the contrary, it is generally believed that this founder of our town, who died in 1769, lies buried here. His great-great-grand-daughter, Mrs. Allen D. Hoffer, told the author that she remembers having visited in her childhood this old graveyard in company with her grandmother, who used to point out an unmarked grave near the western wall as the spot where grandfather Steitz was buried.   But even this is only tradition, however reliable.   Can it be that this old German founder of Lebanon was, like the great leader and lawgiver of Israel, buried by the angels of God out of human sight, and shall no one ever know the place of his sepulture?   The graves of his daughter, grand-daughter and other relatives are here, and their epitaphs are quite legible. There follows that of his grand-daughter, Catharine Reynolds (Clark), to whom he bequeathed his property on condition she marry a German.   But true love neither runs smooth nor according to prescribed lines of nationality, and so this heiress married a Scotch-Irishman, Thomas Clark, Esqr., and I suppose forfeited her legacy.   After a comparatively long and (we suppose) happy life, they were here gathered side by side, and the two large flat marble stones covering their graves give evidence that they were not wholly without means.   Her epitaph reads thus :

In Memory of
Mrs. CATHARINE CLARK
Consort of
Thomas Clark, Esqr.,
who was born on the 29th day
of September 1756
and departed this life
the 30th day of June 1817
Aged 60 years 9 months
and 1 day.

"Blest are the dead whose souls are pure,
Their sufferings past, their glory sure."

The daughter of this couple was the mother of Mr. David Hammond, who, with his family, is to-day numbered among our residents—a direct lineal descent from Mr. Steitz, of quite a number of generations.

Here sleep also the wife and some children of Rev. Dr. Lochman, long the pastor. Likewise the elder Shindels, Embichs, Weidmans, Bickers, Reinoehls, George and Eleanor Reynolds (he a captain in the Revolution, she the only daughter of George Steitz), Schantzes, Sixes, Uhlers, Stoevers and Yensels, besides many others. We give in conclusion a fac-simile of two more epitaphs—those of two children of pastors—the one the youngest son of the first pastor, and the other a daughter of the fourth, whose mother sleeps by her side, having died at 18, when the daughter was a babe of but a year:

Hier Ruhen
Die Gebeinen des
FRIEDERICH STÖVER
Esqr. Ward Gebohren in Libanon
Tausp. Am 20 Sept. A. D. 1759
Und starb
Am 24 May 1833
Brachte Sein alter
Auf 73 Ia. 8 Mo. 4 Da.
Lei 2 Pet. 1 Ca. 1 v.
Joh. L. Stoner Ma.

IN
MEMORY
of
MARIA REIDENAUR
wife of
MR. GEORGE REIDENAUR
and daughter of the
Revd. George Lochman, D. D.,
Died December 7, 1835.
Aged 39 years, 5 months and
2 days.

CHAPTER XXVII.

OUR EXIT VIA OLD CUMBERLAND STREET TO GLONINGER'S FORT.

There is enough of the antique left in Lebanon that has not yet been touched upon in these pages, to keep us busy here for some time longer. But, whilst it would be interesting to hunt up every relic of the preceding century still to be found in the city, it is time that we shake off the dust that has gathered on our travel-worn feet since our halt here and again resume our journey beyond. And so, with thanks for every favor and encouragement received while the guests of the city, my army of explorers, like so many Commonwealers, would graciously bow themselves out and continue their pilgrimage down the lazy windings of the Quittapahilla:

We shall go out orderly, taking the same way that the early visitors to Lebanon took, when making their departure, if their exit was towards the west—up towards Harris' Ferry, later Harrisburg. For let it be remembered that old roads are landmarks as well as old buildings.

Leaving Salem Lutheran church corner and proceeding south on Eighth street, we pass—at the south-east

corner of Eighth and Willow—the home of Mr. John
H. Hoffer, the same building having formerly been
used as a school-house (as well as another old building,
formerly occupying the rear of said lot) in which the
noted Miss Rose Cleveland, sister of the President of
the United States, formerly taught our Lebanon boys
and girls. A little beyond, at the alley, is the Salem
Lutheran parsonage, in and out of which house, or one
formerly occupying the spot, have gone the Lutheran
pastors of this church since the year 1800. Across the
alley from this parsonage is the fine Roman Catholic
church, built in 1876, but which site was previously occupied for 60 years by a chapel, where this congregation worshiped in its infancy. Immediately opposite
is the county Court House—the first erected structure
since the establishment of the county in 1813. This
building was completed in 1818, and ever since that
time our county courts have been held here, where are
kept all the official documents of the same. Some of
the earlier records were supposed to be endangered here
when Lee's army invaded Pennsylvania in 1863, and
were taken to the Schuylkill county court house for
safe keeping, from which they were afterwards returned, and I am told some have not yet been
unpacked from the fugitive packages. Dr. Egle has
published in his history an account of the first court
records, showing that upon the establishment of the
county—the court then held in the fine stone dwelling
on south side of Cumberland street, between 9th and

roth, now owned by Mrs. Boughter—James Buchanan, and Edward Godwin, and Thomas Elder, and Jacob B. Weidman, and the Wrights, and John Marks Biddle, and Edward Coleman, and John M. Forster, and the Fishers, and Hopkinses, and Henry Kurts, and Samuel Laird, and Moses McClain, and William Montgomery, and Nutz, and Morris, and Geo. B. Porter, and Chas. Richards, and the Smiths, and Francis R. Shunk, were among the most prominent attorneys at the bar that practiced here, and that Walter Franklin was the first president judge, and John Gloninger and David Krause were first associate judges.

Diagonally opposite, on the south-east corner of this street intersection, stands the Central Hotel, formerly the old "Buck Hotel," in charge of Joseph Reinhard, where Wm. Henry Harrison stopped during his presidential campaign visit to Lebanon.

Leaving this corner of the city, where the legal business of the county centres, and where every half or quarter of an hour the electric cars of the city meet, let us go westward on Cumberland street. But we shall not take time to do more than point out a few more buildings of note. And one of these is the Ross house, where the flourishing Dr. Ross' drug store is located, noted because this is said to have been the first three-story house erected in the city. What a contrast with that early advanced architecture is the fine Nutting building with its six stories that has recently arisen by its side! Another building which savors of age and has doubtless an interesting history, is the stone building occupied by Shiffler's green-grocery store.

But we cross again the central square and now come to the fine stone dwelling house of Mrs. Boughter. It is very old, but one of the most roomy and hospitably built old mansions in our city. It has associated with it a history that decks it with a new garment of interest, viz: That it was used from the erection of Lebanon county, 1813, until the completion of the court house in 1818, by the county as a temporary court house. It was here that those early legal lights of our court, already mentioned, then practiced law. In its original construction it was built as a farm house and had extensive grounds and all the necessary farm outbuildings. Thus there remained to within a year an old building used as a pig-sty, corn-crib, etc., which is said to have secreted and sheltered for a short time, in the ante-war period, certain fugitive slaves, who, being here befriended, made their escape hence to Canada in safety. To add to the justice and judicial reputation of this old homestead, it might be added that it was the residence at different periods of several legal lights of our court, viz: Jacob B. Weidman, Esq., Levi Kline, Esq., Amos R. Boughter, Esq., and the late Judge of the county, Hon. John B. McPherson.

Immediately opposite this fine old dwelling, where the late C. Henry's residence is now situated, used to stand the public house of Abraham Doebler, where usually stopped the lawyers from other counties that practiced here in that early period. The writer recently learned from one of our best-informed citizens an incident which helps to bring to view the old-fashioned times then lived in this hostlery. The incident was related by Mr. James Buchanan, who told my informant how the loquacious and somewhat officious mistress of this house on one occasion, while he was boarding there, took him (Mr. Buchanan) to a cheaply-drawn portrait of her husband, hanging on the parlor wall, and began to recount the different steps of his successful, self-made career, following the story with an earnest admonition to the young aspirant to be good and self-reliant and persevering in his efforts, and he too might perchance some day shine as brilliantly as her husband. It is said that Buchanan never forgot that advice, and the self-complacent manner in which it was given.

But we must hasten on. The north-east corner of 10th and Cumberland used to contain an old house in which Dr. Marshall of some local fame used to reside. On the south-west corner of this street intersection stands the Farmers' Hotel, which must have been erected more than a century ago. It was built by one Hau Georg Focht, about a decade before the Revolutionary war, inasmuch as this pioneer afterwards moved about four miles east of Lebanon on a farm still in the family's hands, where the house built, prior to 1770 still stands, which date marks the erection of an addition to it a few years later. This Mr. Focht was the great-grandfather of Mrs. John Reinoehl, of our Lebanon.

19

But we come now into the very oldest section of the city, where abound most of the ancient landmarks. Old Cumberland street, which led the way out of town before the Berks and Dauphin turnpike chose another and better way, still contains many of these first buildings. They are mostly low, one story log huts—some

OLD CUMBERLAND STREET, LEBANON, PA.
(Looking east.)

now encased with boards—whose erection must date to the days of Steitz himself. One house here has the tradition of having been used as a church for some time. It is the one numbered "1122," and the shape of the same much resembles the Hebron Moravian Church. It is two-storied, with peaked roof and divided into apartments like the one at Hebron. Was it here that the local Lutherans and Reformed temporarily worshipped before the erection of their first churches in town? Quite likely. For in our last chapter we learned that, because the Lutherans "found the worship of God in private houses inconvenient" they made efforts in 1768 to build a church.

But Steitz! where did he live? There has been much surmise, but as yet we have found nothing more authentic than a tradition that the Uhler residence or "Meadow Bank" of Mr. Geo. Hayes and his family marks the spot. There is much of circumstantial evidence to corroborate this story. It was on the banks of the creek, fronting on the south and east, just the kind of site we always find these old Germans have selected for their homes. Besides, we find here a portion of a very old log building and an arched cellar or cave of such antiquity as to antedate the childhood of our oldest citizens. There is also a tradition that there are logs and beams of a larger building that formerly stood here, used in the construction of the present brick house, built years ago by Mr. Uhler, and that these were said to have been taken from Steitz's old house. Altogether the story is quite probable, and we shall henceforth think that Mr. Steitz spent his American life here, and that a fine meadow along the Quittapahilla stretching before his house (where now the C. & L. trains go to and fro) furnished the best hay for his cattle.

The old Cumberland road (now blocked by the C. &

L. R. R.) used to follow close to the banks of the Quittapahilla creek, at the base of the knoll now crested by Mr. Hammond's fine home (through whose occupant's veins flows the blood of the town's too-much-forgotten and too-little-known founder), and led on through the Gloninger farm, past the old homestead, on to Sunnyside and the Stoever mills. Were we to make a call at Mr. Hammond's palatial residence, we should find it filled with a collection of rare and invaluable family heirlooms, descended through both lines of an equally prominent ancestry.

But we must make a short halt at the Gloninger home in earlier days, commonly known as the Gloninger "Fort." The house is still standing on the south bank of the creek. George Gloninger must have erected it somewhere in the decade between 1740–50. Old histories speak of it as having been used as a place of refuge from the Indians during the period of warfare and their greatest depredations from 1750–65. It is a good specimen of the solid architecture of those days, with its piked roof and original port-holes for windows, and serves as an interesting landmark, because here the first American Gloninger immigrants settled, from whom has descended locally quite an illustrious family. It seems that the names of the American Gloninger ancestors were Peter [Philip(?)] and his wife, Anna Barbara, and that Valentine, John, George and Peter were among their sons. Of these George may have been the oldest and remained on the old homestead as farmer.

The others distinguished themselves in other avenues
of life.   John, born in 1758, took an active part in the
Revolutionary war, rose to official rank, held official
positions in his native (then Dauphin) county by appointment and election, and served a number of years
as Associate Judge upon the erection of the county of

THE GLONINGER "FORT."

Lebanon.   He was married to Catharine Orth, a
daughter of Adam and Catharine (Kucher) Orth.
Their son Philip, born in 1788, was a minister in the
Reformed church, very brilliant, with a promising
future before him, when he was cut down by an un-

timely death in 1816. He had been stationed at Harrisburg previous to his death, and had been married to Eliza Clark, the daughter of Thomas Clark, Esq., and a great-granddaughter of Mr. George Steitz. His widow later married Col. Hammond and became the mother of Col. David Steitz Hammond, who resides in Lebanon. Concerning the ability and fine pastoral spirit of this minister, the following lines written and dedicated by him to his flock and sorrowing friends, a few days before his death, bear ample testimony :

"Meinen Jesum lass ich nicht,
　Jesus wird mir helfen siegen
　Vor dem letzten zorngericht!
　Und hier in den letzten zuegen,
　Ich weiss, nimmt der Tod mich hin
　Dass ich doch bey Jesus bin.

"Wann dich die Last der Leiden drueckt
　Schau drum nicht Muthlos nieder;
　Schau frei empor, sprich, mich erquickt
　Der Herr doch endlich wieder.
　Der Christen hohes Burger-Recht
　Ist dort im Vaterlande.
　Der Christ, der irdisch denkt, denkt schlecht
　Und unter seinem Staude.

"Dort ist das rechte Canaan,
　Wo Lebens Stroeme fliesszen;
　Blick oft hinauf, der Anblick kan
　Dein Leidens-Kelch versuesszen.
　Dort oben ist des Vaters-Haus
　Gott theilt zum Gnaden Lohn
　en Ueberwindern Cronen aus;
　Kaempf euch um Ruhm und Crone.

"Wann ich auch gleich bald scheiden
  Von meinen Freuden soll,
Das, mir und ihn'n bringt Leiden
  Doch tröstet dies mich wohl
Dass wir in groessern Freuden
  Zusammen kommen dort;
Und bleiben ungescheiden
  An einem bessern ort."

Another son of John and Catharine Gloninger was John W., the physician, whose attainments and skill gave him early in his long practice a first rank in the profession. He was a celebrated surgeon and oculist specialist, with a wide reputation. He was a frequent contributor to medical journals, and an honored member of many medical societies. He left a family of children, viz.: Eliza, wife of Dr. David B. Marshall, already alluded to in this chapter; Matilda, wife of John Wetherill, of Philadelphia; Dr. Cyrus D., a noted physician, whose widow and son, (Dr. Andrew H.), now occupy the old residence (corner of 9th and Cumberland); Dr. David Stanley, of Philadelphia, and Alice, wife of Dr. A. H. Light, of Lebanon.

We have recently seen the portrait painting of this old Revolutionary Gloninger worthy, which reflects much of the Saxon honesty, frankness and stern integrity for which he was noted. In the antiquarian collection of our friend, Mr. E. W. S. Parthemore, of Harrisburg, we saw also an honorable discharge from militia duty of a fellow citizen that bears his signature, as follows:

> The bearer, Henry Meyer, of Captain Stover's Company of the Second Battalion of Lancaster County Militia, having made appear to me that he is above the age of 53 years, is discharged honorably from all militia duty, this 19th day of November, 1782.
>
> JOHN GLONINGER, Sec. Lieut. for Lancaster Militia.

Nearly all the Gloningers that have departed this life sleep in the First Reformed Cemetery of this city, in the shadow of the church, which the earliest generations were so active to establish. There we found the graves of Valentine, born June 11, 1766, died December 24, 1844; Peter and Elizabeth, his wife; John and all his family. Fitting monuments, or marble slabs, mark their resting places. Two of these are to the memory of Dr. John W. and Mary Ann, his wife. Another monument has its four faces occupied with memorial inscriptions of the Hon. John, born September 19, 1758, died January 22, 1836 (on the east); his wife, Catharine, born October 31, 1767, died June 17, 1848 (on the west); his son, Rev. Philip, born February 17, 1788, died September 10, 1816 (on the north), and his son Cyrus, born December 25, 1804, died December 22, 1821 (on the south). Suitable epitaphs accompany each.

It is fitting that the memory of such worthy ancestors be preserved, and we trust that whatever improvements may chance to be made in the old Gloninger farm in the hands of the new syndicate, the old homestead may be loug kept as a relic, and that somewhere a park, or street, or institution, may preserve the name of its first white proprietors, as that name is preserved by the far-famed spring that gushes with clearest water from lime-stone rocks on the plantation. To this spring let us now repair, to drink to each other's health as we part company for another interim.

CHAPTER XXVIII.

A VALUABLE LIBRARY HISTORICALLY HOUSED.

"Tread softly here, as ye would tread
In presence of the honored dead,
With reverent step and low-bowed head.

"Speak low—as low as ye would speak
Before some saint of grandeur meek
Whose favor ye would humbly seek.

"Within these walls the very air
Seems weighted with a fragrance rare
Like incense burned at evening prayer.

"Here may we sit and converse hold
With those whose names in ages old
Were in the book of fame enrolled.

"Here under poets' power intense
We leave the world of sound and sense,
Where mortals strive with problems dense,

"And mount to realms where fancy free,
Above our poor humanity,
Roams in a joyous ecstasy.

"Or, if through history's maze we tread,
The hero, patriot, long since dead,
Whose great heart for his country bled,

(290)

"Seems once again to work and fight
In superstition's darkest night
For God, his fellows, and the right.

"Enough! mere words can never tell
The influence of the grateful spell
Which seems among these books to dwell."

So wrote Alice C. Sawtelle in the *Boston Literary World* sometime since ; and we confess being seized by something of this same strange spell upon entrance of any large and well-selected library of books. Of all the apartments of a house, the library has for us the greatest charm. We are ready to confess with Frank Dempster Sherman :

Give me the room whose every nook
Is dedicated to a book:
Two windows will suffice for air
And grant the light admission there;
One looking to the south, and one
To speed the red departing sun.
The eastern wall from frieze to plinth
Shall be the poet's labyrinth,
Where one may find the lords of rhyme
From Homer's down to Dobson's time ;
And at the northern side a space
Shall show an open chimney-place,
Set round with ancient tiles that tell
Some legend old and weave a spell
About the firedog-guarded seat,
Where one may dream and taste the heat:
Above, the mantel should not lack
For curios and bric-a-brac—

Not much, but just enough to light
The room up when the fire is bright.
The volumes on this wall should be
All prose and all philosophy,
From Plato down to those who are
The dim reflections of that star;
And these tomes all should serve to show
How much we write—how little know;
For since the problem first was set
No one has ever solved it yet.
Upon the shelves toward the west
The scientific books shall rest;
Beside them, history; above—
Religion—hope, and faith, and love;
Lastly, the southern wall should hold
The story-tellers, new and old;
Haroun al Raschid, who was truth
And happiness to all my youth,
Shall have the honored place of all
That dwell upon this sunny wall,
And with him there shall stand a throng
Of those who help mankind along
More by their fascinating lies
Than all the learning of the wise.

Such be the library; and take
This motto of a Latin make
To grace the door through which I pass:
Hic habitat Felicitas!

Believing that my readers share with me and others
this subtle charm of the collection of books, we will
spend an hour or more together in looking over the
largest library of rare and antiquarian literature to be
found in this valley. We venture the assertion that

there are not many private collections, and few public
libraries, of greater antiquarian variety in the State,
than that gathered and historically housed by Mr.
Henry S. Heilman, of Sunny Side, whose residence is

MR. HENRY S. HEILMAN'S HOMESTEAD.
A VALUABLE LIBRARY.

about two miles west of Lebanon.   The house in which
he lives is a large and substantial stone structure a century old, and was erected by one of the sons of the
pioneer Lutheran minister of this valley, Rev. John
Casper Stoever.   Two inscribed tablets in its front elevation tell the story and sentiment of its erection as
follows :

Gott Bessegne
dieses Haus und
wer geht da ein
und aus!

———

Johannes Stoever
Angenes Stoeverin
17   95

Friede Sey in
Diesem haus
Und mit Dehnen
Welche Drauss.

———

Dieses Haus
Erbaut ist
Anno 1795

The Heilmans and Stoevers have been intermarried and so this commodious house serves as a relic of these two old families, whose thrift, intelligence and general cleverness have brought esteem and considerable fame to both. The present proprietor of this homestead came into its possession through his father, who died less than a year ago, and into whose possession it came by purchase in 1837. The writer has found him quite hospitable, and so he takes the liberty of ushering his company of fellow-explorers, without further ceremony, right into the room that shelters this antiquarian library, gathered principally by this our host. It is found in the southern wing of this building, on the first floor, to which it was found necessary to build an extension, which reaches back to the very edge of the historic Quittapahilla.

Here are found a sufficient quantity of easy-chairs and rockers to rest the most weary of our historic tramps, while either from a cabinet or a full fledged pipe-organ, we may have our spirits soothed or refreshed with sweet-voiced music ere we begin to ravish our eyes with the contents of the surrounding alcoves of rarest book treasures. All around the wall, from floor to ceiling, stretch the bursting book-cases with their antiquarian lore. Here are gathered some of the oldest and rarest books known to the bibliophile, from the tiniest specimens to the most cumbersome tomes. The library is the complement of Mr. Danner's museum, at Mauheim, of rare china and crockery-ware. That shows the domestic, this the religious life of our people in colonial times. There are here found a number of the cunabulae, or cradle books, and large quantities of the earliest Bibles, and hymn-books, and almanacs, since the art of printing was invented. Among early editions or rare copies of books this library abounds. The Sauers' German Bible of 1743—first editions of Bibles printed in America and very rare—is here represented by three copies. The rarest curios of Franklin's publications here find a place, more especially such specimens of his books as were published for the German people. Among the very rarest books in this collection is one of Conrad Beisel's works, and published in 1730 by Benj. Franklin before even this German Baptist leader could muster strength to have his own press. It is probable that this volume is the only one extant, and Prof. Seidenstecher, before his recent death, had arranged to have the title page of it photographed. We give here this title-page as follows:

Mystische
Und sehr geheyme
Sprueche
Welche in der Himmlichen Schule
Des heiligen geistes erlernet
Und den solgens einige
Poetische Gedichte
Auffgesetzt
Den liebhabern und schulern
Der Goettlichern und Himmlichen
Weisheit zum dienst.
Vor
Die Saü dieser welt aber
Haben wir keine spise werden
Ihnen auch wohl ein werschlossener
Garden und versiegelter brunnen bleiben.
Zu Philadelphia Gedrucht
by B. Franklin im Yahr 1740.

Among the many almanacs collected here, are the *Hoch Americanish Deutcher Kalender*, from 1745 to date, bound in volumes. Two of them were published by Benj. Franklin and called "Neu Americanish Deutscher Kalender." One in 1752, when in September eleven days were dropped or cut out, viz: from the 3rd to 13th inclusive, so as to allow for the difference in time between the Old Style and the New Style of reckoning time, is also found here, and is quite rare. The sum of $100 has been set upon a perfect copy. The full list of almanacs in Mr. Heilman's possession, ranging from 1745 to 1894, all printed in Pennsylvania, is as follows: Those published by Christoph Saur and Michael Billmyer, of Germantown; by Benj.

Franklin, Antony Ambruster, David Caeschler, P. Mueller, Henry Miller, Melchoir Steiner and Carl Cist, Philadelphia ; by Matthias Bartgis, Francis Bailey, Johann Albrecht, of Lancaster, etc., also the family illustrated church almanacs, as the Catholic Home, complete; the Catholic Family, from 1871–76; the Reformed, complete ; Lutheran, incomplete, etc.; also Webster's, Phila. *Record's*, Phila. *Public Ledger's*, the American, Frank Leslie's, Ayer's American in ten languages. All of these are bound and in good condition.

We make a hasty and partial list from memory of other rare and curious volumes we found here, as follows :

1. Almost a complete list of the more than fifty Ephrata publications, some of which are original books, while others are reprints of devotional manuals bearing the imprint of this Seventh Day German Baptist press, including the "Martyrer Spiegel," Ephrata, 1748, which is a volume as large as the largest family Bible.

2. Two copies of the "Poor Man's Bible," being nothing else but a package of slips of German Scripture texts, enclosed in a wooden case —a rare curiosity.

3. A copy of Arndt's *Wahres Christenthum*, reprinted for the German people of Pennsylvania by Benj. Franklin, 1751.

4. "Ein Sermo von den Kleiner Brode," by Dr. *Martin Luther*, gehalten zu Wittenberg in 1523, and printed then.

5. Many of Sauer's publications (Germantown), who was the first American German printer.

6. A manuscript Memorial Reformation Sermon by Dr. F. H. C. Helmuth, in a hand of as perfect German script as if printed—the sermon having been delivered in Philadelphia, Oct. 31, 1817, from text, Ps. cxviii. 24.

7. A voluminous illustrated German copy of Josephus, bearing the

20

imprint of some German publisher, dated 1569—formerly the possession of some German Lebanon Valley settler by the name of Bager Boger, where the celebrated Dr. Demme, Lutheran pastor of Zion Lutheran church, Philadelphia, found it and borrowed it, keeping the same for three years, and using it as a copy for his edition (German) of Josephus, now the one mostly sold to German readers. This old copy has many annotations and corrections on margins, which Dr. Mann has recognized as Dr. Demme's handwriting. [It is said that Dr. Demme and Rev. Ernst were rival candidates for the Lebanon pastorate, but that Dr. Demme's preaching proved too scholarly for these people and Rev. Ernst was chosen, while Dr. Demme went to Philadelphia.]

8. First German Bible printed west of the Alleghenies, at Bedford, with dozens of other rare and old copies of the Holy Scriptures.

9. A copy of Rev. J. Casper Stoever's last will, and other family archives.

This list gives but a faint idea of the treasures that are here collected and carefully arranged. They have cost their possessor no little time, money and research, but they must give him immense satisfaction as they speak to him of the centuries that are past. We can imagine that the encased spirits, communicating from these bookshelves of wisdom's lore are often better companions than many who still wrap flesh and blood about them. So with a courteous bow for favors shown, we shall leave our friend to himself and his mute companions, imagining that we hear him say in the language of John Fletcher:

> Give me
> Leave to enjoy myself. That place that does
> Contain my books, the best companions, is

To me a glorious court, where hourly I
Converse with the old sages and philosophers;
And sometimes for variety I confer
With kings and emperors, and weigh their counsels;
Calling their victories, if unjustly got,
Unto a strict account; and in my fancy
Deface their ill-placed statues. Can I then
Part with such content pleasures, to embrace
Uncertain vanities? No: be it your care
To augment a heap of wealth, it shall be mine
To increase in knowledge.

CHAPTER XXIX.

LET us to-day follow the Quittapahilla Creek for half a mile in its meandering course, from where it washes by the home of Mr. Heilman, last visited, and it will lead us to an interesting relic of the first settlement of this region. It is the old mill-homestead of the Rev. Johann Casper Stoever, the first German Lutheran minister ordained in Pennsylvania. It is located just an eighth of a mile south of the village of Cleóna, and about two and a half miles west of Lebanon. It is a landmark of the olden times that holds for us a fascinating charm.

The building, which is a large and substantial stone mill-structure — originally provided with a suite of domestic apartments, and occupied by this pioneer of Lutheranism as the permanent abode of himself and family for a period of forty years—was erected in the years 1737–40. The strong and substantial character of the building required three years of time to complete it. It is a massive structure, considering the times and the meager facilities of building; in dimensions about 40 by 60 feet. Its walls, three feet thick, are most of them as solid to-day as when first erected, though composed of simple, undressed surface stones, many of them no larger than a man's fist. The mortar is as firm as cement, and no pen-knife has yet been found strong enough to break its cohesive service. The writer has thought that if all the Lutheran stones that first composed the walls of the spiritual building of this denom-

REV. JOHN CASPER STOEVER HOMESTEAD.

ination in America, had been as firmly cemented as this good Lutheran pastor bound together the stones of his earthly abode, this now honored and numerically strong denomination would much sooner have assumed firm and conspicuous proportions in this country.

Whether it was from a generous desire to supply these early settlers with bread for the body as well as for the soul, that this pastor built a mill almost simultaneously with the church, or whether he saw in it a chance to grind more cash into his own pockets, we can not tell and would not wish to insinuate. Suffice it to say that for more than a hundred and fifty years the waters of the Quittapahilla have here turned the machinery that has ground out the one kind of grist for the customer and the other for the owner. It was either the grist of this mill, or that of his large parish, probably both together, that made its first owner comparatively wealthy. For at his death Rev. Mr. Stoever was the possessor, besides this mill-property, of over five hundred acres of the richest land in the valley, which, divided into three large farms, were left to three of his sons, Adam, John Casper (a Captain in the Revolution, whose home we visited last week), and Tobias.

This antiquated pile of masonry, constituting this pioneer minister's earthly abode, was further provided with an arched mural fortification, the foundation walls of which are still visible on the southwest corner of the building. There was also a stockade, or log-barricade, used for defense against savage foes when they made their forays in that period. And here the neighbors were frequently sheltered, when in all this community manifold depredations were committed by the red men.

The illustrious builder of this home was a native of the Electorate of Hesse, now Prussia. There he was born, December 21, 1707, the son of honorable and pious parents. After teaching school for two terms in the Rhenish Palatinate, he sailed from Rotterdam, with ninety of his fellow Palatinates, on the ship "James Goodwill," and landed at Philadelphia September 11, 1728. On the ship's register his name is recorded as Johann Casper Steover, S. S. (Theol. Stud.), and is distinguished from another person of the same name, a near relative, who registered as Missionaire, and settled as pastor of the Lutherans in Spottsylvania, Va. The latter died a few years later at sea, on a return trip from Europe, which he had revisited. The former, after about a year's temporary abode at the Trappe, then known as Providence, Montgomery county, Pa., took up his abode at the Conestoga, near the present town of New Holland, Lancaster county, Pa. Here he lived until about 1740, when he moved to his newly-finished house on the Quittapahilla.

Wherever this young pastor dwelt, he reached out beyond, visiting his scattered conntrymen and organizing them into congregations. Thus we find him in charge of supplying the first Lutheran churches in Montgomery, Berks and Lancaster counties, even before he was ordained. In 1732, Rev. John Christian Shultze, a Lutheran minister ordained in Germany, arrived in this country, and took charge of the congregations at Philadelphia, Providence and New Holland, by which Henry Melchoir Muhlenberg was called ten years later. Shultze early visited Stoever, and being obliged in less than a year to return to England and Germany to secure ministers and money for the relief of Lutherans in Pennsylvania, he ordained Stoever and placed him over these congregations. This ordination took place at the Trappe, in a barn, being the only place of worship this congregation could then afford, and it claims to be the first solemn setting apart to the holy office of a German Lutheran on Pennsylvania territory.

Pastor Stoever must have been a prince at organizing churches. We find his name associated with almost every Lutheran congregation that was founded during the first decade and a half after his arrival in America, in what is now Lancaster, Berks, Lebanon and York counties. At the Trappe, New Holland, Lancaster, Warwick (Brickerville), Tulpehocken, Nothkill (Bernville), Heidelberg (Schaefferstown), Bethel, at Jordan, Krupps, the Hill Church (Berg-Kirch), and at York, his name is associated with the laying of the foundations. Out of these small beginnings have directly grown dozens of strong congregations, and indirectly developed much of the Lutheranism of this State and beyond. For it is quite certain that eastern Pennsylvania is the cradle of the greater portion of American Lutheranism, that to-day numbers its communicants by many hundred thousands.

The organization of the Hill church in 1733, which, however, was long designated as "The Church on the Qui:tapahilla," doubtless led Pastor Stoever to rear his home near it. Hence, having built this abode he removed hither from the Conestoga in about 1740, and here raised his family.   Here transpired what is of domestic interest for more than the latter half of the long life of this enterprising and energetic dominie. There are two incidents of peculiar interest associated with this ancient landmark.   The one is the friendly hospitality shown a fellow pastor and his family upon their arrival here from the Fatherland. This family was no less a one than that of the Rev. John George Bager, the first American progenitor of the well known Baughers of the Lutheran Church. When this ancestor, after a brief pastorate in Simmern, Germany, arrived with his small family in Philadelphia, October 23, 1752, Pastor Stoever, by previous arrangement we presume, was there to meet him and take him to his own home "on the Quittapahilla." Here the new-comers were hospitably quartered for eight months.   Meanwhile (June 9th, 1753) the third child was born unto these recent immigrants, which was named Catharine Margaret, and at whose baptism by Pastor Stoever, the dominie's wife and hostess stood as sponsor.   Rev. Bager had meantime received and accepted a call as pastor from the Lutheran church of Hanover, Pa., which he served for three months before removing his family from this hospitable abode.   It is worthy of mention in this connection that by a singular and happy coincidence, two descendants of these friends and yoke-fellows were afterwards intimately associated as co-workers in the early history of Penn-

sylvania College at Gettysburg—the one in the person
of Dr. Henry Louis Baugher as professor of Greek and
as President of the institution for a period of thirty-six
years, and the other, Prof. Martin Luther Stoever,
LL.D., as principal of the preparatory department and
as professor of history and Latin in college for a period
of twenty-eight years.

The other incident alluded to is that connected with
Pastor Stoever's death. Although feeble and sickly for
years prior to his demise, this energetic servant of God
did not unbuckle his gospel harness until the end came.
His debilitated condition, however, sometimes incapacitated him to leave his house, when, if possible, he
sought to minister to his people there. Thus he had
requested his catechetical class of the Hill church to
meet him at his home on Ascension Day (May 13th,
1779), anxious that they be confirmed on that day in
order to be ready to participate with the congregation
in the celebration of the Lord's Supper on the coming
Whitsuntide. Accordingly the class here convened, and
after a lengthy and fatiguing service of review and examination, concluding with the rite of confirmation, the
pastor, utterly exhausted, fell over and expired in the
presence of his family, some members of his flock and
the class upon whose heads he had just laid the hands of
confirmation. His funeral took place a few days later
at the Hill church, where in the adjoining graveyard his
ashes repose. It is possible that the near future will see
a fitting monument rise here to do honor to a life so

abundant in labors and so self-sacrificing and heroic in its efforts to help and befriend others.

Before taking our leave of this interesting old mill-manse—now the property of Henry S. Heilman, who in 1879 purchased it of a Mr. Shenk, and soon thereafter undertook to make some internal repairs—let me say that much of the building's interior and exterior is as it was in the days of Stoever. ' Tis true, the domestic apartments have been torn out or altered, but the windows, the floors, the walls, all the main framework of the building remains. If the same waterwheel is not there, the same creek still supplies the power to carry on the same business. Immense timbers constitute the frame-work. From a heavy poplar beam that was removed at its remodeling, the writer has had carved for himself at the Miller Organ Company, of Lebanon, a beautiful relic in the shape of a tray and goblets. On a two-inch walnut step was, until recently, found the name of the builder, together with the date 1737, evidently burned on with a hot iron. The hat-rack of Pastor Stoever, of walnut framework and pegs, upon which he must have hung his great-coat or hat a thousand times and more, is still preserved. So are some of the library and closet-doors of the old manse, all made of solid walnut. Altogether, the landmark is well preserved and well worth a visit by any one interested in what is so fraught with ancient and important events.

CHAPTER XXX.

A VISIT TO HILL CHURCH.

LET us take our walk to-day with the pioneer Lutheran dominie of this valley, from his mill-manse on the Quittapahilla last visited, to the church on the hill ("Berg-Kirche"), about a mile to the northwest. As we walk in the olden time it will not be difficult to imagine this pious pastor as accompanying us, for this is a journey he regularly made for nearly forty years prior to his death, and before the Revolution. There was not a little danger connected with church-going here when this first pastor was yet officiating, for we have records that frequently the people were obliged to bring their guns along to be ready to defend themselves against the attacks of the savages.

This church is the mother of all Lutheran and Reformed congregations in this vicinity. Whether it was Reformed from the very beginning the writer cannot positively assert, but we find both branches of these oft-united portions of the German Protestant church worshiping here as early as 1744. From a history of the churches in Lebanon county, given by Dr. Geo. Lochman in 1812, we learn that the congregation was gathered as early as 1733, and is the oldest church in

(308)

the county. According to its earliest records kept, it was called the "Church on the Quittapahilla," though it seems now quite a little distance from this stream.

The first building consisted of a rudely constructed edifice of logs. There were also hewn logs for seats,

THE HILL CHURCH ("BERG KIRCHE").

and a most primitive construction served as pulpit. The building had no floor, and there were in it no stoves for a long time, according to the prevailing custom of the warmer clime of the native country of these German worshippers. In the coldest wintry months a wood-fire of logs was built on the outside of the church, around which the assembled congregation would sit awaitiug the arrival of the miuister. Even when the congregation could well afford such a luxury as a wood-stove, its introduction is said to have met with considable opposition. There was a rack provided for storing away their guns during worship, though frequently a few of the members stood as weaponed sentinels at the church doors while worship was being conducted. The present brick building was erected in 1837, it being the third edifice.

The following Lutheran pastors have served this church :

Rev. John Casper Stoever, 1733-1779.
Rev. Frederick Theodore Melsheimer, 1779-1794.
Rev. George Lochman, D. D., 1794-1815.
Rev. William G. Ernst, D. D., 1815-1836.
Rev. Jonathan Ruthrauff, 1836-1849.
Rev. A. C. Wedekind, D. D., 1850-1853.
Rev. J. M. Deitzler, 1856-1860.
Rev. Christian A. Fetzer, 1860-1863.
Rev. George P. Weaver, 1863-1864.
Rev. J. M. Dietzler, 1865-1890.
Rev. W. H. Lewars, 1890-date.

The Reformed pastors have been the same as those who served the First Reformed Church of Lebanon (see record), beginning with Rev. Conrad Templeman as early at least as 1744, if not 1733; and after the church of Lebanon became an independent pastorate, in 1864, the Hill church was connected with the Annville pastorate, and has since been served by Dr. Jonathan E. Hiester.

The early Lutheran record, kept by the first pastor, is quite complete. The book in itself is a curiosity, being bound in raw-hide and its leaves worm-eaten and greatly discolored by age. Still the entries are quite legible and should be published in some form to be preserved. We give this gentle hint to the present pastor, in whose hands it is found. There is here also quite an old Bible, printed in Halle more than a century ago, and bought by the congregation for the altar service (in which use it is still found), for 16 shillings and 6 pence. So there is likewise in possession of the church a very old Communion cup, bearing date 1745.

Being located on high ground there is here afforded a magnificent view of the rich valley that stretches out before the visitor, while just beyond the ridge to the north nestles the lovely vale of the Heilmans, from which surrounding farms (among the loveliest of this entire valley) there gathers Sabbath after Sabbath a goodly congregation and Sunday-school of intelligent and enterprising farmers to worship God and perpetuate the work of the church established by their pious and heroic ancestry, sleeping here in the adjoining "God's acre."

The graveyard which surrounds the old church abounds in old graves, whose epitaphs read in our day like pages of ancient history. Yet in many instances the same family-names are found on the church record to-day that are chiseled also on these old tomb-stones. Here are buried such old families as the Bohrs, Bogers,

Bensons, Blacks, Bechtels, Barths, Boltzes, Cleiiners,
Detweilers, Embichs, Fochts, Fishers, Gingrichs,
Heilmans (a large number), Imbodens, (a branch of
which family drifted to Virginia and was represented
on the Confederate side in the late war by General
Imboden), Killingers, Kellers, Kelkers, Karmanys,
Kurtzs, Kleins, Millers, Matters, Rupps, Reinoehls,
Richerts, Rutters, Stoevers, Schnebeles, Sprechers,
Umbergers, Ulrichs and Xanders.

Among the oldest graves many epitaph inscriptions
have become illegible. That of the first Lutheran
pastor has been retraced by the sculptor's chisel, and is
therefore clearly discernible. It is somewhat as follows:

Hier Ruhet
In Seinem Erlöser Entschlaffen
JOHANN CASPAR STOEVER
Erster Evangel Luthericher Prediger
in Pensilvanien. ist geboren in
Der under Pfalz D. 21 Dec. 1707. Er
zeigte mit seiner Ehe Frau
Maria Catharine 11 Kinder 4 sein
in die ewigkeit voran gegangen,
Er Starb D. 13 May 1779. Seines Alters
71 y. 4 mon. 3 wo. v. 2 Tag.

By the pastor's side sleeps his wife, Maria Catharine, who survived him a number of years; near by rest a number of their children and later descendants. The Rev. Henry Wagner, one of the Reformed pastors, was also buried here in 1869, but a few years since his relatives had his body exhumed and re-interred in the Mt. Lebanon cemetery.

Here sleep also the American ancestors of the Kelkers and Heilmans, both prominent and rather numerous families of the Lebanon Valley. Fitting stones were erected to mark the spot of their burial as late as 1867, by devoted and thoughtful descendants of their respective families. The Hon. Rudolph F. Kelker, of Harrisburg, a great-grand-son of this early Swiss immigrant, was instrumental in so fittingly marking his worthy ancestor's grave. The stone, of the Hummelstown red sandstone quarry, in massive proportions, reads as follows :

"In Memory of
Henry Kolliker (Kelker),

Born in 1705. Emigrated from Herrliberg, Canton Zurich, Switzerland, and settled in Bethel (now Swatara) township, Lebanon county, in 1743. One of the Elders of the Reformed congregation, Hill Church, in 1745. Died 1762. Also Regula Braetschert, his wife."

This worthy descendant has also compiled and published an interesting "Family Register," giving a long and careful genealogy of this family in Switzerland and America.

The stone that here marks the resting place of the

21

first American Heilman ancestor is similar in size and quality to the one just described. It is in memory of John Adam Heilman, born November 16, 1715, in the Palatinate, who emigrated to America in 1738, here married Maria Catharine Steger (of the family then living near Avon, as previously alluded to), who became the progenitors of at least a very large branch of the Heilman family in Lebanon county. This John Adam Heilman was in 1745 a fellow-elder with Mr. Kelker on the Reformed side of this Hill Church, and he died September 25, 1770.

One of the oldest tombstones here is a curiosity for the elaborate ornamentation of rosettes, skull and cross-bones upon it and the fact of its being engraved on both sides, the one containing the obituary quite minute, and the other several verses of the solemnly warning German hymn, beginning:

"Komm, Sterblicher betrachtig mich,
Du lebst, ich lebt auf Erden,
Was du jetzt bist das war auch ich,
Was ich bin wirst du werden."

The name of the person buried is, however, scarcely legible, but looks like Johann W. Hefs. "Ist gestorben im Jahr Christy 1754. Ist gebohren in Jahr 1722 den 27ten Mertz und den 29 darauf getauft worden auf die Evangelische Lutherische Religion, &c., &c." The stone is found some distance directly back of the church.

The writer thinks that there is history enough here
to deserve its preservation and the perpetuation of the
good influences that have emanated from this spot, by
the erection of a new church of stone, after some beautiful, artistic model, with stained-glass windows to tell,
in legends and pictures, the story of struggle and piety
that associates with this sacred spot. There is wealth
enough in the congregation to build that church now.
There should be enough devotion to religion and
family pride enough to keep this enterprise from a long
delay.

Another thing that this place deserves is a fitting
monument to the memory of now the only, but heroic
pastor who sleeps here—the Rev. J. Casper Stoever. If
the performance of a multiplicity of great and important labors ever deserved such a mark of reverence and
respect, then truly the self-denying labors of this man of
God, laboring for forty-six years in the establishment of
this, and many other churches of Pennyslvania, deserve
such distinction. We are happy to note that the present Lutheran pastor is making efforts to accomplish
this end, and we trust that these efforts will meet with
a hearty response and be crowned with speedy and
glorious success. [P. S. See next chapter.]

CHAPTER XXXI.

THE STOEVER MONUMENT.

WHAT was hinted at toward the close of the last chapter has, since its first writing (1894), materialized. Through the efforts of the pastor, Rev. W. H. Lewars, considerable interest has been manifested in the matter of placing a fitting monument over the sacred dust of the pioneer pastor, who sleeps upon the historic hillock of the "*Berg Kirche,*" so that, in the near future, the devout wishes of a few local antiquarians are about to be consummated. Upon next Ascension Day, the anniversary of Rev. Stoever's death, is to be unveiled this beautiful marble shaft. The material of this monument (which is the finest quality of blnish-tinted marble) was quarried at the historic Horse-shoe pike, in the heart of this valley, from the quarry operated by Messrs. J. H. Black and C. S. Maulfair, themselves chips of the sturdy block of Lutheran ancestry that settled here in Stoever's time, and which was spiritually sculptured by his gospel hammer and chisel in that early day. The famous Lebanon county sculptor, Mr. J. H. Black, of Annville, has carved the monument, as seen in the accompanying cut, by which we are enabled, through the courtesy of Rev. Lewars, to show our readers the design of this memorial shaft.

It is anticipated that an immense throng of people
will congregate here on the day of the unveiling; as this

event has been made to be simultaneous with the Convention of the Lebanon Valley Lutheran Sunday-school
Association and a meeting of the Lebanon Conference

of the East Pennsylvania Synod of the Lutheran Church, under whose auspices the unveiling and dedication will take place.

The Program Committee has asked the author of these historic sketches to read a poem on this occasion, which, as the publication of this book will so nearly coincide with this about to become historic event, he will here append. Other important addresses will be delivered by members of Conference and by other celebrities of the church.

THE STOEVER MEMORIAL.

BY REV. P. C. CROLL.

The Muse's wand is in my hand,
  To use it I've discretion,
Can let its spell on this large band
  Work thoughts into expression;
Or let it wake the preacher dead,
Who sleeps within yon lowly bed,
In honor of whose pastorate
This congregation now has met.

And so I'll use the poet's Muse
  To summon forth this sleeper;
From Chronicles his text I'll choose;
  His theme—The Grave my Keeper.
And of the past I'll make him preach,
Back o'er a hundred years he'll reach,
To tell us here in simple rhymes
Of Gospel work in pioneer times.

So now give ear, the preacher's here,
  Arisen from his slumbers;
He casts his eyes far out and near
  Astonished at the numbers
Who came from far to hear him preach,
Who used their great-grandsires to teach
The principles of truth and right
In days that tried men's souls aright.

He looks to see who each can be
  Who came to hear his sermon,
But cannot quite himself agree
  If you are Hans or Herman.
He sees resemblance to that fold
That worshiped here in days of old,
Yet still his look is strangely wild
Till told you're Hans' great-grandchild.

But now the spell comes o'er him well,
  His heart becomes inspired;
His tongue is glib the tale to tell,
  His soul with zeal is fired;
To teach the children of this day,
Who've met in such a vast array,
The hardships of that dreadful day
When men here used to "watch and pray."

His voice is heard, forth flows his word,
  'Mid earnest intonation:
" Beloved children in the Lord,
  Who form this congregation,
Why meet on this Ascension day
And leave your muskets home, I pray?
Have you not feared the Indians' snare,
The panther's fierceness, nor the bear?

"And tell me what became of that
   First church of logs and sheeting,
Those racks for flint-locks, coat and hat,
   Those hewn-log paws for seating?
Pray, who has torn that pulpit down?
And who has ripped my cleric-gown?
And who has lit those coals of fire,
'Stead looking for some warmth up higher?

"Who could not brook the old hymn-book?
   Why don't you sing in German?
What's given you this English look?
   Who's Anglicized my sermon?
Since I have laid me down and slept
An English flood has o'er you swept;
Your blood is mixed, as well your speech—
The Anglo-Saxon stamp's on each!

"And where are now, on hillock's brow,
   Those forest trees primeval?
Who cleared these acres for the plow?
   Who tills them without equal?
A Rip Van sleep I must have slept
While yonder stone its vigil kept,
And marked my resting-place, 'neath sod,
In this blest acre of our God!

"Then let me tell—all marking well—
   My antiquated story,
How, ere your sires to warfare fell
   'Gainst Briton and 'gainst Tory,
The early settlers of these parts,
With Church and Bible near their hearts,
Reared here an altar to their God,
Whilst felling trees and turning sod.

" And here they swore, those years of yore,
  Heart fealty to Jehovah,
Who brought them to this Western shore
  In arks secure, like Noah.
And while they drew a breath on earth,
Themselves, with all their goods and worth,
They gave to God an offering,
Though claimed by George, the English king.

" Across the same great sea I came
  And landed in you city,
That still proclaims, in deed and name,
  A brother's love and pity ;
Thence up the Schuykill's boisterous waves,
And where the Conestoga laves,
I visited my countrymen
To cheer their German hearts again.

" Soon came a cry from far and nigh,
  Like Macedonian pleader,
Our German folk for help did sigh,
  For Gospel and for leader.
And thus I journeyed o'er the land,
From Jordan's to Codorus' strand,
Till on the banks of th' " Quitopehille "
I built my house within a mill.

" From that abode for years I rode
  In rain and shiny weather,
In seasons when the streams o'erflowed—
  My horse swam like a feather—
I brought the story of the cross—
For none then took account of loss—
To those who fled to 'scape the sword,
And settled here to serve the Lord.

"And now appear around me here
  Those heroes' later offspring,
Prepared a monument to rear
  In mem'ry of my off'ring.
I can't rebuke my children dear
For that which must to all appear
A deed that's prompted by the good,
And gives for nobler thoughts some food;

" But I would fain that every name
  Of elder and of deacon,
And others working just the same
  To light this gospel beacon,
Would stand engraved on yonder stone,
And over all, above, alone,
Old Luther's watchword, so well put :
'*Ein feste Burg ist unzer Gott!'* "

CHAPTER XXXII.

A GLIMPSE OF ANNVILLE.

LET us come down now from the hillock upon which have worshiped for one hundred and sixty years the pious German settlers of this portion of the valley that is watered by the Indian-famed, *snake-harboring* Quitta-pahilla, and let us get a glimpse of the little gem that adorns this magnificent vale. Like a sparkling diamond upon the bosom of a king, so the neat little aggregation of houses, and schools, and churches, and workshops, and business houses, known as Annville, formerly as Millerstown, begems the bosom of this Quittapahilla valley. From whatever side you approach it, it charms and glitters. It has inherent beauty as a rural town, and needs no outside adornments to make it attractive. Whether viewed from the northern ridge of hills or the southern valley of its bordering creek, whether you walk through its streets or approach it from the east or the west, it is the same "sleeping beauty"—not a Sleepy Hollow—in this season of the year a veritable bride, adorned in her virgin summer robes, and decked off to charm the lover-husband who has espoused her and made her his own. Its many peaceful looking homes, lovely in architecture, and surrounded by velvety lawns and gratefully disposed shade-trees ; its towering church

spires and its imposing college buildings, surmounted
with classic-looking cupolas and classic-ringing bells,
and surrounded by an umbrageous campus, combine to
make Annville an ideal town in picturesque beauty
and in all the attractions of rural municipality. A pity
it is that it is not owned by itself, but still belongs to
the surrounding townships. I should think it had
reached its majority, and was able to cut the maternal
apron-string and start out in life independently. If it
does this, and adds a few more tucks to its maiden frock,
it can soon boast of being the prettiest municipal daughter of all this Lebanon valley, and such a launching out
upon the municipal world would doubtless add to the
list of its devout admirers.

This town was laid out by one Miller shortly after
the middle of the last century, and for a number of
decades was named Annville, but afterward Millerstown
for a long period, when because of its confusion in
postal matters, it was again changed to the first name
about a generation ago. Messrs. Abram Raiguel and
Ulrich have also taken leading parts in the town's early
establishment. Some of the original houses are still
standing on its main and side streets. But there is no
particular history connected with them, save that doubtless into them entered that famous impostor—Dr. John
Dady—that sacerdotal wolf-in-sheep's-clothing, who in
the latter portion of last century, here for a while suc-
cessfully practiced a smart game of gulling the simple, all too credulous German folk and extorting their

hard-earned cash from them. This glib-tongued Hessian—a remnant of those contemptible English Revolutionary hirelings—however, was not sharp enough to hide, for a long period, his black and greedy heart under his ministerio-medical coat from the Argus-eyed officer of the law, who in due time discovered his deception, tore the mask from his face, and sent him to the penitentiary, where he deservedly pined out his life. For further data concerning this impostor we refer the reader to Rupp's History of Berks and Dauphin counties.

Another dark page to blot the otherwise fair history of this fair village is the monstrous deed of infanticide of "old Showers." This is of such recent date that it need not be recounted here. The buildings where this foul deed was committed, and where the murderer lived, and other scenes connected with the horrible acts here transacted, are still found in the southern portion of the town, while murderer and murdered sleep close together in one of the burial grounds of the town, awaiting their resurrection and final judgment at the "last day."

About the oldest landmark of historic account is the old Ulrich homestead to the northeast of town, almost opposite the Reading railroad depot. The place is now the home of Mrs. Commodore P. Steinmetz's family, suddenly bereft of father and husband not long ago. Here early in the last century the first Ulrich immigrant settled, the great-grandfather of Mrs. Steinmetz, and in 1751 he built a stone house, part of which is still standing.   It was provided with an arched cellar, built over a never failing spring, and with air-holes, being thus furnished with the essentials for life, and proved a safe place for retreat in case of an attack by the

THE OLD ULRICH HOMESTEAD.

Indians, as happened on several occasions.   That these early inhabitants must have realized their constant and imminent danger to life from this source is evinced by the engraving found upon the stone that was used as the door-sill of the old fort, viz.:

"SO OFT DIE THÜR DEN ANGEL WENDT,
O MENSCH, DEIN END BEDENK! 1751."

This stone is still found here, but when the house was remodeled it became part of a porch-pillar, while a newly-engraved head-stone preserves the old legend in more modern and legible form, together with the names of the builders, Mr. and Mrs. Steinmetz. This old house was used as a store and trading post with the Indians by the first Ulrich; and the apple orchard, just in front of the homestead, is pointed out as an Indian burial ground, for it is reported that many Indians made their home for weeks with this first white settler. One evening this pioneer and his son (the father of the the late Adam Ulrich) were surprised by an attack of a murderous gang of red-men, but were fortunate enough to escape their deadly tomahawks and scalping-knives, by a hasty retreat to this sheltering refuge-cellar, where-upon the maddened savages killed all their cattle by cutting out their tongues. This happened about the year 1756 or 1757. If we mistake not, this is the place also where the Rev. Daniel Ulrich, of Tulpehocken fame, was born and reared to manhood.

Walking through the town, one is struck with the classic-looking grounds and buildings of the Lebanon Valley College of the U. B. Church, located here, under the successful management of Dr. Bierman, president ; the tasty-looking homes, the fine churches, the well-built and well-painted public houses or hotels, enter-prising carriage manufactories of John L. Saylor and Sons, Barnhart and Beam, T. Loser and Mr. Shenk, the long-established and reliable marble works of J. H.

Black, the Daisy Shirt Factory, carried on by a stock
company, of which the late Judge Kinports was first
president (present incumbent is not known to the
writer), the lime-stone pulverizing works of John Bachman, and the three ancient grist-mills on the banks of
the Quittapahilla. These are now in the proprietorship
of Messrs. John Bachman, David Kreider and Long &
Himmelberger (owned by Mr. Killinger of Lebanon), respectively, commencing on the east and following the
stream in its westward course. The principal stores of
town are in the proprietorship of Messrs. Kinports and
Shay, Beam and Bachman, M. F. Batdorf and John
Shope. The first store kept here was that of the late
Mr. John Shertzer, who came to this village in its infancy from Manheim, and made quite a fortune in his
time. The building used for the prosecution of his
business is now used by the Annville Fire Insurance
Company, and owned by C. Smith, Esq.

Walking south on White Oak street, one passes a
number of buildings with an interesting local history.
One of these is the fine stone residence of Mr. William
Biever, ex-County Treasurer. This used to be the
residence of his uncle, Mr. John D. Biever, who was
one of Annville's most liberal and public-spirited men
in his day. Besides the furthering of other laudable
enterprises, he was in a sense the founder and father of
the first Evangelical Lutheran church located on Main
street. Besides donating the ground, he paid about
one-half of the cost of building, presented the church

with a fine two-story brick sexton's house, made provision (which his widow carried out after his death) of erecting an elegant and commodious brick parsonage next to the church, and endowed the church to the

CHURCH BUILDING, PARSONAGE, AND SEXTON'S HOUSE OF THE FIRST EVANGELICAL LUTHERAN CHURCH AT ANNVILLE, PA.

amount of $3,000. His widow supplemented this amount by an additional legacy of $2,100, while the same estate endowed the cemetery by another $1,000. The present pastor of this church, Rev. W. H. Lewars, says, concerning these benefactions and this noble-hearted man: "It is but due to say, that the commendable generosity here recorded grew out of a life-long Christian character. The piety of Mr. Biever was acknowledged by all who knew him. He assumed a directing and sustaining influence in the church for half a century, and for forty-nine years was the superintendent of the Sunday-school." The house in which Mr. Biever lived was built by his father, John D. Biever, Sr., in 1814.

In the year 1804 was erected the substantial stone church edifice located on this street, on a little elevation of ground and shaded by a grove of locust trees. It was originally built as a union church (Reformed and Lutheran), and is a child of the Hill church. It has been exclusively Reformed since 1871. Its pastor, Rev. Dr. Hiester, has served it consecutively for forty-two years, and we are told there is a vigor about his preaching to-day that would indicate that not much of his natural force has as yet abated. The other Reformed pastors that have served this church were the same as have preached at the Hill church during this period. The Lutheran pastors have been Revs. Lochman, Ernst, Krotel, Miller, Porr, Fetzer, Weaver and Deitzler. The school-house, as is customary, we find near the church, but since the days of the public school system it has been remodeled and used as a residence. It is at present occupied and owned by Mr. Daniel Seabold. Here such teachers as Messrs. Fisher, Bachman, Strine and others taught the now gray-headed citizens of the town and their departed companions during their juvenile years, the Psalters and their German spelling-books.

Strolling on past the old cemetery, we soon come where the cool and mill-wheel-turning Quittapahilla flows by the town.   A beautiful stone triple-arched bridge here spans the stream, from which one has a picturesqueness of view in the new surrounding land-

THE RAIGUEL MILL.

scape that is quite charming.   Close by is the old mill of Abram and Elizabeth Raiguel, which, according to the date-stone in its front elevation, was built A. D. 1797.   On a little hillock to the south stands the fine old Raiguel farm-house, with all its antique appurtenances, built four years earlier, a venerable centennial

relic of rural comfort, agricultural prosperity and that
proverbial peace and contentment that attend husbandry.
Here, if we mistake not, the wife of Rev. Dr. A. C.
Wedekind, of San Diego, Cal., and Mrs. Boughter, her
sister, of Lebanon, were raised to womanhood. The
Cassidys and Shirks have also married into this family.

THE RAIGUEL FARM-HOUSE.

This farm, with its ancient dwellings, is now the
property of Mr. Josiah Kreider, living near the Horse-
shoe pike, while the mill property has been owned
since 1840 by David Kreider and his son, present
proprietor. All of this property, and many acres
besides, was the original possession of Abram Raiguel, a

bachelor uncle of the builder of the mill named, whose log cabin used to stand where the farm-house now stands. He was a native of Cougmont, Switzerland, from whence, after settlement here, he called his nephew and made him his heir. Other old families are the Imbodens (one scion the Confederate General from Virginia), Kreiders, etc., all whose first ancestors are buried at the Hill church.

Were we to drift down this Indian-named creek we should soon come to where, in the days of the Revolution, stood a gun-barrel boring mill, an adjunct, we suppose, to the very prosperous gun-smith business which then flourished in and about Lebanon. Farther down we would find the grist-mill of Mr. Killinger, built long ago by a Mr. Herr, and still farther · on its course the spot where, in 1812, Mr. Hentzleman and others of Lancaster county, erected, at the enormous expense of $96,000, an extensive cotton and woolen factory, which failed in due time, according to Rupp, only because of the "ruinous policy of the non-protection of American industry."

Were we to drift on in our imaginary course, we should shortly arrive where this stream mingles with the waters of the Swatara. And here we can imagine seeing those other rude rafts, or canoes, on which were embarked the wives and children of the sixty families of temporary Scholiarie settlers, who, in the spring of 1723, were passing this point, making slow progress up this stream towards its headwaters and that of the Tulpehocken, their longed-for destination. What better place than this to close our historic pilgrimage, and here suffer the streamlet of our explorations to be engulfed by the mightier tide of our common history? Therefore, we shall bring our ancient and historic researches to an end on the banks of this valley's most conspicuous stream, of which and whose settlers the gifted Whittier has sung as early as 1836, when he addressed his "Lines" to Governor Ritner of our State, as follows:

> "And that bold-hearted yeomanry, honest and true,
> Who, haters of fraud, give to labor its due:
> Whose fathers of old sang in concert with thine,
> On the banks of Swatara, the songs of the Rhine,
> The German-born pilgrims, who first dared to brave
> The scorn of the proud in the cause of the slave."

www.ingramcontent.com/pod-product-compliance
Lightning Source LLC
Chambersburg PA
CBHW021122270326
41929CB00009B/1005